The Life and Ministry of Paul
An Inductive Bible Study

LeRoy Curtis

FOREWORD

The Life and Ministry of Paul is part of a sixteen course curriculum of inductive study that includes the entire Bible. It was originally designed in 1990 to teach indigenous pastors in developing countries to read and understand the Bible for themselves. **Basic Inductive Bible Studies (BIBS)** formed the core of the diploma program used by The Kenya Ministry Training Institute to prepare church leaders to proclaim the Gospel more clearly. I have since used this curriculum in the local church in the United States to enhance a deeper understanding of Scripture and how it is interpreted.

The inductive approach starts off with answering the question, "What does this passage say?" Usually that is fairly clear. Sometimes we need a Bible dictionary or Lexicon to help us with difficult words. The next question, "What does this mean?" can be a little more complicated. As I learned in Africa and Latin America, different cultures have diverse worldviews and can lead to conclusions that might seem strange to those who are indoctrinated in Western Intellectualism. I have learned much by patiently listening to the rationale that leads other people groups to different conclusions than my own. Revelation is an extra-rational phenomenon. God reveals His truth in unique ways through the power of His Holy Spirit. Mystery is always involved whether our intellect approves of that, or not. When we humbly share revelation with others, always asking the question, "What is God saying to us?" a creative dialogue is initiated. The dialogue, in turn, refines individual revelation into a clearer picture of what a scripture means. Corporate revelation guards us from distortions and unnatural interpretations of biblical passages. The last question, "What must we do now that we understand this passage? is the most important one. Application of the Scriptures in our lives is the whole point of knowing them in the first place. Conforming to God's will as expressed in the Bible is our goal. We want to be doers of the Word, and not hearers only.

While this study can be profitable for lone individuals, I would recommend that it be pursued with at least two others to get a fuller and more complete understanding. A living dialogue about God's Word has amazing consequences. It creates an atmosphere of worship as revelation opens our eyes to the wisdom of the Lord and we discover his awesome eternal plan for creation. **Basic Inductive Bible Studies** can be used in many and various situations. It can be used in churches as part of an integrated study program for adults or youth. It would serve well as the foundation for a Christian high school Bible curriculum with some additional writing assignments added. Over the years it has proven to be a valuable tool for training bi-vocational pastors who cannot leave their churches for formal Bible School training. Any group of people who want a better grasp of Scripture could utilize these studies to guide them.

To get the most from this course some serious study is necessary. The many questions may seem tedious and overwhelming, but they are asked so that you are required to closely examine the text instead of merely casually scanning the words as we are prone to do. You will be surprised how much information is there that can be easily missed and how important details can be to our understanding.

This study begins with certain important assumptions about the Bible. The foundational principle is that Jesus Christ is Lord of all creation and the Head of the Church. The Scripture teaches us who he is and what he does. It lays out the Gospel message of hope for all who trust in him. The second major principle is that the Bible is the true Word of God, and our final authority in all matters of faith and Christian practice. We study the Bible so that we may become more like our Lord in our daily lives. The final principle is that, apart from the Holy Spirit, we have no capacity to understand God. Our study is in vain without his intervention and inspiration. All revelation flows from God's sovereign grace and love extended to his people. Thankfully, it is his will that we know him and through his revelation we may have eternal life.

I have used the New International Version (NIV) of the Bible as the basis for this and every course in the Basic Inductive Bible Studies (BIBS) curriculum. There was no particular theological reason for doing so. I have no issues with any of the major translations. They are all based on solid scholarship and each has its own particular merit. I chose the New International Version merely because it is widely available nearly everywhere. Other versions may be used with this study, but not without difficulty in answering some of the questions simply because the phraseology may be different.

I sincerely hope and pray that this study will help you better understand God's eternal purposes and bring you to a closer relationship with him. God bless you.

LeRoy Curtis

e-mail: leroy.judy@gmail.com

Note: The cover contains an image of Saint Paul, painted by El Greco about 1614.

Table of Contents

Lesson One
I. PAUL'S BIRTH THROUGH HIS FIRST VISIT TO JERUSALEM

A Paul's Background

1. His heritage
   a. Paul was a Jew.
      1) Acts 21:39
      2) II Corinthians 11:22)

   b. Paul was from the tribe of Benjamin.
      1) Romans 11:1
      2) Philippians 3:5

   c. Paul was born in Tarsus of the Province of Cilicia.
      1) Acts 21:39
      2) Acts 22:3
      3) Acts 23:34

2. His education
   a. Paul was taught the Law by Gameliel. (Acts 22:3)

   b. From youth he was trained as a Pharisee.
      1) Acts 23:6
      2) Acts 26:4-5
      3) Philippians 3:5

   c. Paul was exceedingly zealous. (Galatians 1:14)

3. His character
   a. Paul was zealous and righteous. (Philippians 3:6)

   b. He blasphemed and persecuted the Church out of ignorance and unbelief. (I Timothy 1:13)

   c. He had a clear conscience. (II Timothy 1:3)

B. Saul, Persecutor of the Church

1. Saul participated in Stephen's stoning.
   a. The witnesses left clothes with Saul.
      1) Acts 7:58
      2) Acts 22:20

b. Saul consented to Stephen's death.
   1) Acts 8:1
   2) Acts 22:20

2. Saul participated in the persecution of the Church.
   a. He imprisoned Christians.
      1) Acts 8:3
      2) Acts 22:5
      3) Acts 22:19
      4) Acts 26:11

   b. He beat Christians. (Acts 22:19)
   c. He testified against them in their execution. (Acts 26:10)
   d. He pursued them abroad.
      1) Acts 22:5
      2) Acts 26:11

C. Paul's Conversion

1. The Damascus Road experience
   a. Saul was on the way to continue persecuting Christians.
      1) Acts 9:1-2
      2) Acts 22:5

   b. Saul had a "heavenly vision."
      1) At noon he saw a bright light from heaven.
         a) Acts 9:3
         b) Acts 22:6
         c) Acts 26:13

      2) Saul fell down.
         a) Acts 9:4
         b) Acts 22:7
         c) Acts 26:14

      3) Jesus spoke to Saul, asking why Saul was persecuting Him.
         a) Acts 9:4-5
         b) Acts 22:7-8
         c) Acts 26:14-15

      4) Saul asked who Jesus was, and for instructions.
         a) Acts 9:5
         b) Acts 22:10

5) Jesus told Saul to go to Damascus for further instructions.
   a) Acts 9:6
   b) Acts 22:10

6) Saul became blind.
   a) Acts 9:8-9
   b) Acts 22:11

2. There were reasons why Jesus appeared to Saul:
   a. To make him an apostle (one who has seen Jesus face to face)
      1) I Corinthians 1:1 - Paul called to be an apostle.
      2) I Corinthians 9:1 - Paul asks if he is not an apostle, if he has not seen the Lord.
         ("Yes" is the obvious answer.)
      3) I Corinthians 15:8 - Paul claims to be the last to see Jesus.
      4) Galatians 1:1 - Paul claims to be an apostle made by Jesus Christ, not by men.
      5) Romans 1:1 - Paul says he was called to be an apostle, separated unto the Gospel of God.

   b. To make him a minister and witness (Acts 26:16)
   c. To help people turn from darkness and the power of Satan to light to receive forgiveness of
      sins and sanctification by faith (Acts 26:18)

3. Saul's experience in Damascus
   a. Jesus appeared to Ananias, a devout disciple in Damascus, and told him to go look for Saul to
      heal him of his blindness. (Acts 9:10-12)

   b. Ananias resisted because of Paul's fearful reputation. (Acts 9:13-14)

   c. Jesus reaffirmed that He has chosen Paul for a special purpose. (Acts 9:15-16)

   d. Ananias ministered healing to Saul and commissioned him into ministry.
      1) Acts 9:17
      2) Acts 22:13-15

   e. Paul was filled with the Holy Spirit and was baptized.
      1) Acts 9:17-18
      2) Acts 22:16

D. Paul's Early Ministry (37-39 A.D.)

   1. Paul stayed in Damascus
      a. He preached immediately.
         1) Acts 9:20
         2) Acts 26:19-20

      b. Paul amazed the believers, and confounded the Jews. (Acts 9:21-22)

2. Paul went to Arabia. (Galatians 1:17 - perhaps to fast and pray)

3. Paul returned to Damascus for three years. (Galatians 1:17-18)

4. Paul escaped Damascus to Jerusalem.
   a. Acts 9:23-26
   b. II Corinthians 11:32-33

5. Paul's First Visit to Jerusalem (39 A.D.)
   a. He stayed with Peter for 15 days. (Galatians 1:18)
   b. The disciples were afraid of Paul. (Acts 9:26)
   c. Barnabas testified in Paul's favor. (Acts 9:27)
   d. Paul spoke boldly in Jerusalem. (Acts 9:27-29)
   e. Jesus warned Paul to leave. (Acts 22:17-21)

E. Paul Continues to Preach (39-45 A.D.).

1. Paul left for Caesarea and Tarsus. (Acts 9:30)

2. He preached in Syria and Cilicia. (Galatians 1:21-24)

3. He probably planted churches there among Gentiles. (Acts 15:23;Acts 15:41)

4. Barnabas Begins to Minister with Paul
   a. He was sent out to Antioch and sought Saul in Tarsus. (Acts 11:19-25)
   b. Paul and Barnabas spent a year teaching the church at Antioch. (Acts 11:26)
   c. Paul and Barnabas brought alms to Jerusalem. (Acts 11:30)
   d. Paul and Barnabas brought John Mark back from Jerusalem. (Acts 12:25)

Lesson One
Study Questions

1. In which town and province was Paul born?

2. From which tribe did Paul come?

3. Who was Paul's teacher?

4. To which sect (party) of the Jewish religion did Paul belong?

5. What reasons did Paul give for persecuting the Church?

6. In what ways did Paul participate in Stephen's death?

7. Why should the Christians have feared Paul?

8. Where was Paul going when he had his vision?

9. Why do you suppose the vision happened at noon?

10. Why do you suppose Jesus blinded Paul?

11. What happened to Paul in Damascus?

12. How was Paul's conversion (being saved) like yours, and how is it different?

13. What was most important about Paul seeing Jesus?

14. Why did Paul leave Damascus?

15. Who did Paul stay with in Jerusalem?

16. Who helped Paul in Jerusalem?

17. How did Paul know he should flee Jerusalem?

18. Who came looking for Paul in Tarsus?

19. Where did they go?

    What did they do?

    How long?

20. Why did they return to Jerusalem?

21. Who did they bring back with them?

Lesson Two

II. PAUL'S FIRST MISSIONARY JOURNEY (45-49 A.D.), Reference Acts 13:1-14:28

A. Paul and Barnabas Were Chosen and Sent. (Acts 13:1-3)

  1. They were sent by prophets and teachers from the church at Antioch.
     a. The prophets and teachers had been ministering to the Lord and fasting.
     b. The Holy Spirit spoke to the group instructing them to send Saul and Barnabas.
     c. They fasted and prayed.
     d. They laid hands on Saul and Barnabas and sent them off.

  2. Paul And Barnabas Went To Cyprus. (Acts 13:4-12)
     a. They were sent by the Holy Spirit.
     b. They sailed from Seleucia (near Antioch) to Salamis on the Island of Cyprus.
       1) At Salamis they preached the Word of God in the synagogues (Jewish meetings).
       2) John Mark was with them to help.

  3. They went across the Island to Paphos.
     a. They met Bar-Jesus, the sorcerer (also known as Elymas).
       1) He was a Jew.
       2) He was a false prophet.
       3) He was a friend of the proconsul (Sergius Paulus).

     b. Sergius Paulus called for Saul and Barnabas.
       1) He wanted to hear the Word of God.
       2) Elymas tried to turn him away from the faith.

     c. Paul (Saul) rebuked Elymas.
       1) Paul was (first) "filled with the Spirit."
       2) He called Elymas "son of the devil."
       3) He said he was turning God's truth into lies.
       4) He cursed Elymas with blindness.

     d. Sergius Paul believed.
       1) He saw what happened.
       2) He was greatly amazed.

  4. They sailed from Paphos to Perga in Pamphylia. (Acts 13:13)
     a. John Mark left them and went back to Jerusalem.
     b. This fact became a problem later.

B. Paul and Barnabas Went to Antioch of Pisidia (not the same place they left). (Acts 13:14-52)

  1. Paul spoke in the synagogue.
    a. After reading of scripture
    b. Upon being invited by the officials
    c. He gave a brief history of Israel (God's chosen people).
    d. He said Jesus was the Savior God had promised Israel.
    e. He told about John's ministry.
    f. He explained how Jesus was condemned, crucified, and buried, but was raised from the dead.
    g. He explained that the good news was for them today:
      1) Forgiveness of sins was for them.
      2) Those who believe would be set free from sin which the Law of Moses could not do.
      3) He warned them against unbelief.

  2. Paul and Barnabas were invited back the next Sabbath.
    a. Many Jews and converts followed them after the meeting.
    b. Paul and Barnabas encouraged them to live in God's grace.
    c. Nearly the whole town came to the next meeting to hear the Word of the Lord.
    d. The Jews became jealous.
      1) Because of the crowds
      2) They disputed Paul.
      3) They insulted Paul.

    e. Paul and Barnabas spoke boldly to the Jews.
      1) They said it was necessary to speak to the Jews first. (Romans 1:16, Acts 3:25-26)
      2) They said the Jews did not consider themselves worthy of eternal life.
      3) They said they would go to the Gentiles (non-Jews).
        a) This was in obedience to the Lord's command. (Isaiah 49:6)
        b) The Gentiles were glad and praised the Lord's message.

    f. Those who had been chosen for eternal life became believers.
    g. The Word of God spread everywhere in that region.

  3. Paul and Barnabas were thrown out of the region.
    a. Jews stirred up the chiefs and important women of the city against them.
    b. Persecution against them started.
    c. Paul and Barnabas shook the dust off their feet in protest against them.
      (Jesus' command, Matthew 10:14)
    d. They left for Iconium.
    e. Believers in Antioch were full of joy and the Holy Spirit.

C. Paul and Barnabas Went to Iconium. (Acts 14:1-6)

  1. The same problem occurred in Iconium.
    a. Paul and Barnabas spoke at the synagogue
    b. Many Jews and Gentiles became believers.

c. Non-believing Jews stirred up the Gentiles against the believers.

2. The apostles (Paul and Barnabas) stayed there a long time (probably a few months).
   a. They spoke boldly about the Lord.
   b. The Lord proved that their message about His grace was true by giving them the power to perform miracles and wonders.
   c. The people of the city were divided.

3. Some Gentiles and Jews with their leaders decided to mistreat the apostles and stone them.
   a. When the apostles learned about it they fled.
   b. They went to the city of Lystra and Derbe in Lycaonia and the surrounding territory.

D. Paul and Barnabas Continued to Minister at Lystra. (Acts 14:7-20)

1. They preached the good news.
2. Paul healed a lame man.
   a. He had been crippled from birth.
   b. Paul saw his "faith."
   c. Paul commanded him to stand on his feet.

3. The people then thought the apostles were gods.
   a. They believed Barnabas to be Zeus, whose temple was near, and Paul to be Hermes, the chief speaker.
   b. They tried to make a sacrifice to them.

4. Paul and Barnabas stopped the people from making a sacrifice to them.
   a. They tore their clothes to show distress.
   b. They ran to the middle of the crowd.
   c. Paul announced that:
      1) They were humans.
      2) They were there to announce the good news.
      3) They were there to turn the people away from worthless things to the living God.

   d. The apostles still were barely able to stop the people from sacrificing to them.

5. The Jews came from Antioch of Pisidia, and Iconium and won the crowds.
   a. They stoned Paul (Paul mentions this in II Corinthians 11:25).
   b. They thought he was dead.
   c. They dragged him out of town.

6. When the believers gathered around Paul (to pray?), he got up and returned to town.
7. The next day Paul and Barnabas left for Derbe.

E. Paul and Barnabas Went to Derbe, Lystra, Iconium, and Antioch. (Acts 14:21-25)

  1. They preached the good news at Derbe and won many disciples.

  2. They returned to Lystra, Iconium, and Antioch of Pisidia.
    a. They strengthened believers.
    b. They encouraged them to remain true to the faith.
    c. They taught that we must pass through many troubles to enter the Kingdom of God.
    d. They appointed elders in each church:
      1) They prayed and fasted.
      2) They commended elders to the Lord.
      3) They trusted the Lord.

  3. Passing through Pisidia, they came to Pamphylia.
    a. They preached in Perga.
    b. They went to Attalia.

F. Paul and Barnabas Return to Antioch of Syria. (Acts 14:26-28)

  1. They gathered the church together and reported what God had done among the Gentiles and how He had opened the way for the Gentiles to believe.

  2. They stayed a long time there with the believers (two years, 48-49 A.D.).

  3. Paul Made Comments Later About His First Missionary Journey. (II Timothy 3:10-11)
    a. He mentioned his longsuffering (endurance).
    b. He mentioned his persecutions at Antioch, Iconium, and Lystra.
    c. He stated that the Lord rescued him from all of them.

Lesson Two
Study questions

1.   Who sent out Paul and Barnabas?

2.   How did they know to send them?

3.   In what way were they sent out?

4.   Where did Paul and Barnabas go from there?

5.   What did they do at Salamis?

6.   Who was Bar-Jesus (Elymas)?

7.   What happened to him?

8.   Why did this happen to him?

9.   Who was Sergius Paulus?

10.   Why did he believe?

11.   What happened in Perga?

12.   Who allowed Paul to speak in the synagogue at Antioch of Pisidia?

13.   How did the people first respond to Paul's message?

14. Who came to the next meeting?

15. Why did they come?

16. How did the Jews react?

17. What did Paul and Barnabas say they would do?

18. Who became believers at Antioch?

19. What was the result of Paul's preaching there?

20. How did Paul and Barnabas respond to being thrown out of the Pisidia region?

21. Where did they go next?

22. What happened there?

23. How did the Lord prove the apostle's message was true?

24. Why did the apostles flee?

25. Where did they go next?

26. What happened at Lystra to make the people think Paul and Barnabas were gods?

27. What reasons did Paul give for being there?

28. Who caused Paul to be stoned?

29. What did Paul and Barnabas do in Derbe?

30. At which churches did they appoint elders?

31. What, according to the apostles, must we pass through to enter the Kingdom of God?

32. In what scripture does Paul mention the persecutions of his first missionary journey?

33. How did Paul get through his persecutions?

34. Where did Paul and Barnabas end this journey (the first missionary journey)?

Lesson Three
III. THE FIRST CHURCH COUNCIL IN JERUSALEM,
AND PAUL'S RETURN TO ANTIOCH OF SYRIA (Acts 15:1-35)

A. Paul and Barnabas Were Sent to Jerusalem. (Acts 15:1-3; Galatians 2:1-2)

1. Men from Judea (Jews) came to Antioch saying, "You can't be saved unless you are circumcised as the Law of Moses requires." (These men are known as "Judaizers.")

2. Paul and Barnabas argued with them.

3. It was decided that Paul, Barnabas, and some others would go and see the apostles and elders about the matter.
   a. Titus was taken along. (Galatians 2:1)
   b. Paul said it was revealed by God that Paul should go. (Galatians 2:2)

4. They reported the success of the gospel among the Gentiles as they passed through Phoenicia and Samaria; believers were happy to hear this.

B. The Meeting at Jerusalem (Acts 15:4-29, Galatians 2:2-10)

1. Paul and Barnabas arrived in Jerusalem. (Acts 15:4)
   a. Paul's group was welcomed by the church, the apostles and the elders.
   b. They gave a report about God's work though them.

2. Paul had some private interviews. (Galatians 2:2)
   a. He communicated privately to them (apostles and elders) of the reputation of the gospel he was preaching.
   b. He wanted to protect his work from failure.

3. There was public discussion about circumcision. (Acts 15:5; Galatians 2:3-5)
   a. Pharisee believers insisted that Gentiles must be circumcised and obey the Law of Moses.
   b. Titus (a Greek, **not** a Jew) was not forced to be circumcised, although some wanted it done. (Galatians 2:3-4)
      1) These Judaizers were pretending to be fellow believers.
      2) They were spies on Paul's freedom in Christ.
      3) They wanted to enslave believers (to the Law of Moses).

   c. Paul's group resisted in order to keep the truth of the gospel safe for true believers. (Galatians 2:5)

4. The meeting of the Council was held. (Acts 15:6-29; Galatians 2:6-10)
   a. Apostles and elders met together to consider the question.
   b. There was a long debate.
   c. Peter spoke first, and said: (Acts 15:6-11)
      1) He was chosen once by God to preach the gospel to the Gentiles.
      2) God showed approval to Gentiles by giving them the Holy Spirit as well as to Jewish believers.
      3) God made no difference between Jew and Gentile; both purified by faith.
      4) Why test God by requiring them to obey the Law of Moses when Jews could not even do it?
      5) Jews believe and are saved by the grace of the Lord, just as the Gentiles are.

   d. Barnabas and Paul gave their report of the miracles and wonders God had performed through them among the Gentiles. (Acts 15:12)

   e. James spoke next: (Acts 15:13-21)
      1) God shows He cares for the Gentiles by taking from them a people belonging to Him.
      2) The words of the prophets are in agreement:
         a) I will return says the Lord. (Amos 9:11-12)
         b) I will restore the Kingdom of David.
         c) The rest of mankind will come to me.
         d) All the Gentiles whom I have called to be my own will come.

      3) We should not trouble the Gentiles who are turning to God.
      4) Instead, write them a letter telling them:
         a) Eat no food offered to idols.
         b) Abstain from sexual immorality.
         c) Eat no animals which have been strangled.
         d) Consume no blood.

5. Delegates were chosen to return to Antioch with Paul and Barnabas. (Acts 15:22) They included:
   a. Judas Barsabbas
   b. Silas (called Silvanus later in the epistles)

6. A letter was sent to the Gentiles. (Acts 15:23-29)
   a. The letter had greetings from apostles and elders.
   b. It said that those troubling the Gentiles had no instructions from the apostles and elders to do so.
   c. It advised that messengers were being sent with Paul and Barnabas:
      1) Judas and Silas
      2) They will tell you in person the contents of the letter.

   d. The apostles and elders said that the Holy Spirit and we agree not to put any unnecessary rules on you; necessary rules include:
      1) Eating no food offered to idols
      2) Consuming no blood

3) Eating no animal which has been strangled
4) Abstaining from sexual immorality

e. They said, "You will do well to avoid these things; farewell."

7. Paul later taught about the "necessary" rules for Gentile believers:
   a. Romans 14:14 - No food is unclean in itself.
   b. I Corinthians 8:8 - There is no gain or loss in what we eat or don't eat.
   c. I Timothy 4: 4-5 - Nothing is to be rejected.
   d. I Corinthians 6:18 - We should flee from sexual immorality.
   e. I Corinthians 10:8 - We must not be guilty of sexual immorality.
   f. Colossians 3:5 - You must put to death earthly desires at work in you
      such as sexual immorality.

8. Paul and Barnabas' mission to the Gentiles was authorized. (Galatians 2:6-10)
   a. The leaders made no new suggestions to Paul.
   b. They saw that God had given him the task of preaching the gospel to the Gentiles like He had
      given Peter the task of preaching the gospel to the Jews.
   c. By God's power Paul was made an apostle to the Gentiles as Peter was to the Jews.
   d. The leaders, James, Peter, and John recognized Paul's special task.
   e. The leaders shook hands with Paul and Barnabas as a sign that all were partners:
      1) Paul and Barnabas would work among the Gentiles.
      2) James, Peter, and John would work among the Jews.

   f. The leaders asked Paul and Barnabas to remember the poor in Jerusalem.

C. Paul and Barnabas Went to Antioch. (Acts 15:30-36, Galatians 2:11-14)

   1. The letter was delivered to the church. (Acts 15:30-33)
      a. The messengers gathered the groups of believers and read the letter.
      b. When the letter was read, the people were filled with joy.
      c. Judas and Silas (who were prophets) said much to encourage and strengthen the brethren.
      d. The messengers were sent back in peace to Jerusalem after "some time."

   2. Paul and Barnabas stayed in Antioch for a while and, together with many others, taught and
      preached the Word of the Lord.(Acts 15:35)

   3. Paul had a quarrel with Peter. (Galatians 2:11-14)
      a. Peter came to Antioch.
      b. Paul opposed Peter in public.
      c. Peter ate with Gentile brothers until some men sent by James arrived (they were Jews).

d. Peter stopped eating with Gentiles:
  1) He was afraid of the "circumcision group."(Judaizers)
  2) Others, even Barnabas, became afraid to eat with the Gentiles.

e. Paul saw that this is not "acting in line" with the truth of the gospel.
f. Paul asked why Peter wanted to force Gentiles to follow Jewish customs.

Lesson Three
Study Questions

1. What was the teaching of the men from Judea?

2. Did Paul and Barnabas agree with them?

3. What was decided about the matter?

4. Who was one of the others who went?

5. Why did Paul later say he went?

6. How did the believers in Phoenicia and Samaria respond to Paul and Barnabas' report?

7. What three things did Paul think of those who wanted every believer to be circumcised?

8. Why did Paul's group resist the "circumcisers"?

9. According to Peter, how did God show His approval to Gentile believers?

10. According to Peter, how are both Jew and Gentile purified?

11. What prophet does James quote concerning the Gentiles?

12. What was James' opinion?

13. In what ways can Christians today trouble those who are just turning to God now?

14. What four things did James think Gentile Christians should avoid?

15. Who was chosen to go back to Antioch with Paul and Barnabas?

16. Who sent the letter about the Council's decision to the Gentile churches?

17. Why is that important?

18. Whose opinion did the apostles accept?

19. According to his later writings, to which of these "necessary rules" did Paul agree?

20. In what other passage of scripture is the meeting in Jerusalem mentioned?

21. With whom did Paul compare his work?

22.   What was the agreement between Paul and the apostle leaders?

23.   Did Paul seem afraid of the apostles?

24.   In what way did he see himself as Peter's equal?

25.   What did the messengers do when they got to Antioch?

26.   How did the people respond to the message?

27.   What ministry did Judas and Silas have?

28.   What did Paul and Barnabas do in Antioch?

29.   Why did Paul rebuke Peter?

30.   How did Paul describe Peter's actions?

Lesson Four
IV. PAUL'S SECOND MISSIONARY JOURNEY (51-54 A.D.) (Acts 15:36-18:23)

A. Paul and Barnabas Separated. (Acts 15:36-41)

  1. They decided to visit every town in which they had preached to see how the brothers were getting along.
  2. Barnabas wanted to take John Mark.
  3. Paul didn't want to take him because he had deserted them at Pamphylia.
  4. An argument caused them to separate.
    a. Barnabas took Mark to Cyprus.
    b. Paul chose Silas and left.
      1) They were commended by the believers to the care of the Lord's grace.
      2) They went through Syria and Cilicia, strengthening the churches.

B. Timothy Joined Paul. (Acts 16:1-5)

  1. Paul (and Silas) went to Derbe and Lystra.
  2. At Lystra Paul found Timothy.
    a. He was a Christian.
    b. His mother was a Jew, his father a Greek.
    c. All believers in Lystra and Iconium spoke well of him.

  3. Paul circumcised Timothy.
    a. He did it because of the Jews.
    b. They knew Timothy had a Greek father.

  4. They went through the towns.
    a. They delivered to the believers the rules decided upon by the apostles and elders.
    b. They told them to obey those rules.

  5. The churches were strengthened, growing in numbers daily.

C. Paul's Vision (Acts 16:6-11)

  1. Paul's team went through Phrygia and the region of Galatia.
  2. They were forbidden by the Holy Spirit to preach in the province of Asia.
  3. At the border of Mysia, Paul's team tried to go into the province of Bithynia.
    a. The Spirit of Jesus did not allow them.
    b. They went through Mysia and went to Troas.

4. Paul had a vision.
   a. A Macedonian was begging for them to come and help.
   b. He got ready to go to Macedonia.
   c. Paul decided God had called them to preach the gospel there.

5. Paul's team left Troas and went to Neapolis by way of Samothrace.

D. Paul Went to Philippi. (Acts 16:12-40, Philippians 4:2-3)

1. Paul spent several days at this city.
   a. It was in Macedonia.
   b. It was a Roman colony.

2. On the Sabbath Paul's team went out from the city.
   a. They went to the riverside.
   b. Jews gathered there for prayer.
   c. They talked to the women who were there.

3. They met Lydia from Thyatira.
   a. She was a dealer of purple cloth.
   b. She worshiped God.
   c. The Lord opened her mind to what Paul was saying.
   d. She and the people of her house were baptized.
   e. She asked Paul's team to stay at her house if they thought she was a true believer.

4. Paul's team in Philippi included:
   a. Silas (Acts 16:19)
   b. Timothy (Acts 16:1-3)
   c. Luke (Acts 16:11) - note Luke, author of Acts, uses "we" for the first time
   d. Euodia (Philippians 4:2-3) - a woman who labored with Paul in the gospel
   e. Syntyche (Philippians 4:2-3) - a woman who labored with Paul in the gospel
   f. Clement (Philippians 4:3) - a fellow worker
   g. Others not mentioned ("The rest of my fellow workers")

5. A slave girl was healed.
   a. The team was on the way to pray when they met a slave girl.
      1) She had an evil spirit.
      2) The spirit enabled her to predict the future.
      3) She earned a lot of money for her owners by telling fortunes.

   b. The girl followed Paul.
      1) She shouted, "These men are servants of the most high God," and "they announce to you how you can be saved."
      2) She did this for many days.

c. Paul became upset and cast out the evil spirit.
   1) He cast it out in Jesus' name.
   2) It left the girl immediately.

d. The owners of the girl seized Paul and Silas.
   1) They realized their profit was gone.
   2) They dragged Paul and Silas to the Roman officials in the public square.
   3) They charged them with causing trouble:
     a) Because Paul and Silas were Jews.
     b) Because Paul and Silas were teaching customs against Roman law.
     c) Because the people couldn't accept those customs.

   4) The crowd joined the attack on Paul and Silas.

6. Paul and Silas were beaten and imprisoned. (Acts 16:23-24, I Thessalonians 2:2)
   a. The officials tore off Paul and Silas' clothes and had the men beaten.
   b. They were thrown into prison.
   c. The jailer, under orders, locked them in an inner cell and fastened their feet in blocks.
   d. They were mistreated and insulted. (I Thessalonians 2:2)
   e. Paul considered this incident a struggle. (Philippians 1:30)

7. There was an earthquake at the prison. (Acts 16:25-34)
   a. Paul and Silas were praying and singing praises to God.
      1) This happened at midnight.
      2) The other prisoners were listening.

   b. There was a sudden, violent earthquake.
      1) It shook the foundations of the prison.
      2) All the doors opened.
      3) All the chains fell off the prisoners.

   c. The jailer woke up.
      1) He saw the doors opened.
      2) He thought prisoners had escaped.
      3) He started to kill himself.

   d. Paul shouted to him:
      1) He shouted at the top of his voice.
      2) "Don't harm yourself."
      3) "We are all here."

   e. The jailer rushed in and fell trembling at the feet of Paul and Silas.
      1) He led them out.
      2) He asked, "What must I do to be saved?"

f. Paul and Silas told him, "Believe in the Lord Jesus, and you will be saved - you and your household."

g. They preached the Word of the Lord to him and all the others in the house.
1) The jailer then washed their wounds.
2) He and his family were baptized at once.
3) He fed Paul and Silas at his house.
4) He and his family were filled with joy, because they now believed on God.

8. Paul and Silas were released by the officials. (Acts 16:35-40)
a. An order was sent to release Paul and Silas.
1) The jailer informed them.
2) He told them to go in peace.

b. Paul refused to leave; he said:
1) They were beaten without a trial.
2) They were imprisoned.
3) They were Roman citizens.
4) The officials must release them publicly.

c. The officials apologized and led them out of prison.
1) They were afraid when they heard Paul and Silas were Roman citizens.
(Note: It was against Roman law to punish a citizen without a trial.)
2) The officials asked them (nicely) to leave the city.

d. Paul and Silas left prison.
1) They went to Lydia's house.
2) They met the believers there.
3) They spoke words of encouragement to them.
4) They then left the city of Phillipi.

E. Paul Went to Thessalonica. (Acts 17:1-9, I Thessalonians 1:1-2:16; 3:7-13; 4:9-10, II Thessalonians 1:2-12; 2:13-17; 3:1-14, Philippians 4:16)

1. He came to Thessalonica.
a. He passed through Amphipolis and Apollonia.
b. In Thessalonica there was a synagogue of the Jews.
1) Paul held discussions for three Sabbaths.
a) He quoted and explained scripture.
b) He proved from the scripture that the Christ had to suffer and rise from the dead.
c) He proved that Jesus was the Christ.

2) Some of them believed.
a) Some joined Paul and Silas.
b) Many of the leading women joined.
c) A large group of Greeks who worshiped God also joined.

2. The Jews became jealous.
   a. They rounded up some bad characters.
   b. They started a riot.
   c. They attacked Jason's home.
      1) This was an attempt to find Paul and Silas.
      2) They wanted to bring them out to the people.

   d. When the Jews couldn't find Paul and Silas, they dragged Jason and other believers before the city authorities.
      1) They shouted, "These men have caused trouble all over the world."
      2) "Now they have come here."
      3) "Jason has welcomed them into his house."
      4) "They are all defying Caesar's decrees."
         a) They are saying there is another King.
         b) They say his name is Jesus.

3. The charges threw the crowd and authorities into an uproar.
4. Jason and the others were required to pay bond and were released by the authorities.
5. Paul supported himself in Thessalonica (I Thessalonians 2:9; II Thessalonians 3:6-14; Philippians 4:16)
   a. His team worked hard as they preached the gospel.
      1) They worked night and day.
      2) They did not want to be a burden to the believers there.

   b. Help came from the church at Philippi. (Philippians 4:16)
   c. Paul and his party were an example to the Thessalonians. (II Thessalonians 3:7, 9)
      1) They were not idle (lazy).
      2) They paid their own way.
      3) They worked day and night so as not to be a burden to anyone.
      4) They worked, although they had a right to demand support.
      5) Paul later said, "Whoever refuses to work should not be allowed to eat." (II Thessalonians 3:10)
   d. Therefore, Paul instructed the church to avoid brothers who are living the lazy life and not following his instructions.

6. Paul worked faithfully in Thessalonica. (I Thessalonians 1:9-2:12)
   a. He was well-received.
      1) People turned from idols to serve God.
      2) They began to wait for Jesus' coming.
      3) They wanted to be rescued from the coming wrath of God.

b. Paul's visit was not a failure.
   1) He was mistreated in Philippi.
   2) He was opposed in Thessalonica.
   3) But, God gave him encouragement to preach the gospel.

c. Paul always spoke as God wanted him to:
   1) His appeal was not based on error.
   2) He did not have impure motives.
   3) He was not trying to trick anyone.
   4) He was judged as worthy to be entrusted with the Word of God.

d. Paul tried to please God:
   1) Because God tests the motives.
   2) Paul didn't try to please men.
      a) There was no flattering talk.
      b) There was no disguised greed.
      c) There were no attempts for praise.

e. Paul was gentle with the Thessalonians.
   1) As an apostle, he could have made demands, but didn't.
   2) Paul was like a mother taking care of her children.
   3) His love made him ready to share his life with them, as well as the gospel.
   4) He sacrificed in order to preach the gospel to them.

7. The life and faith of the Thessalonians was apparent. (I Thessalonians 1:1-8; 2:13-16; 4:9-10)
   a. They put their faith into practice.
   b. Their love made them work hard.
   c. Their hope in the Lord was firm.
   d. They became an example to all believers in Macedonia and Achaia.
      1) God loved them and chose them.
      2) The Good News was brought with power and the Holy Spirit.
      3) The Good News was brought with complete conviction of the truth.
      4) They followed the example of Paul and the Lord.
         a) They suffered much.
         b) They received the message with joy from the Holy Spirit.
      5) God was at work in them.
      6) They loved their fellow believers.
   e. Both the message about the Lord and the news about their faith went out everywhere.
   f. They received the gospel as God's message.
   g. Their persecution and suffering was comparable to that of the church in Judea.

8. Paul later cared for the Thessalonians. (I Thessalonians 2:17-20; 3:1-5)
   a. Paul wanted to return.
    1) He was separated from them for a little while:
      a) Not in thoughts, only in person
      b) He missed them (longed to see them).
      c) He tried more than once to return, but was hindered by Satan.

    2) They were his pride and joy.
      a) They were his hope.
      b) They were his joy.
      c) They were his reason for boasting of his victory in the presence of the Lord Jesus when He comes.

   b. Paul sent Timothy back to the Thessalonians.
    1) He was sent to strengthen them.
    2) He was sent to help their faith in persecution.
      a) Persecution was forewarned.
      b) Persecution is part of God's will for us.

    3) He was sent to find out about their faith.

F. Paul Went to Berea (Acts 17:10-15, I Thessalonians 2:17-20; 3:1-5)

1. The believers sent Paul and Silas to Berea at night.
2. They went straight to the synagogue when they arrived (as always).
   a. The people were more open-minded than in Thessalonica.
   b. They listened with great eagerness.
   c. Every day they studied the scriptures to see if Paul was preaching the truth.
   d. Many of them believed, including:
    1) Prominent Greek women (of high social standing)
    2) Greek men

3. The Jews from Thessalonica came to Berea.
   a. They heard Paul and Silas had preached the gospel there.
   b. They started stirring up and exciting the mobs.

4. The believers immediately sent Paul to the coast.
   a. Silas and Timothy stayed in Berea.
   b. Paul was taken to Athens.
   c. Paul instructed Silas and Timothy to join him as soon as possible.

G. Paul Went to Athens. (Acts 17:16-34)

1. Paul was distressed over the many idols in the city.

2. Paul held "discussions" (reasoned with the people):
   a. In the synagogue with the Jews
   b. With God-fearing Greeks
   c. In the marketplace every day with passers-by
   d. With a group of Epicurean and Stoic philosophers (teachers)

3. There was confusion about what he was saying.
   a. Some called him a babbler (ignorant showoff).
   b. Others thought he was talking about foreign gods because he was teaching about Jesus and the resurrection.

4. The philosophers took Paul before the Aeropagus (Mars Hill), the name of the City Council.
   a. They wanted to know about Paul's new teaching.
   b. The people in Athens liked spending all their time telling and hearing new things.

5. Paul spoke to the Council.
   a. He said that Athenians were religious.
      1) He found many places and objects of worship.
      2) He also found an altar to an "unknown god."

   b. Paul said the "unknown god":
      1) Is the maker of the world and everything in it
      2) Is the Lord of heaven and earth
      3) Doesn't live in man-made temples
      4) Gives life, breath, and everything else to everyone

   c. Paul said that from one man God made all the nations (or races) and made them live throughout the earth.
      1) God did this so men could seek Him,
      2) And perhaps find Him because He is close.
      3) In Him we:
         a) Live
         b) Move
         c) Have our being (exist)
      4) We are His offspring (children).

   d. Paul said that since we are God's children:
      1) We shouldn't think that He is anything like an image of gold or silver or stone.
      2) We shouldn't think that He has been shaped by the design and skill of man.
      3) He has overlooked the times of men's ignorance.

   e. Paul said now God commands all people everywhere to repent:
      1) For He has set a day in which He will judge the world.
      2) He will judge by means of the justice of a man (Jesus) He has chosen.
      3) He has proved this fact to everyone by raising Him from the dead.

6. The people heard Paul.
   a. Some sneered at him.
   b. Some wanted to hear more.
   c. A few became followers and believed, including:
      1) Dionysius, a Council member
      2) Damaris, a woman
      3) A number of other people

H. Paul Went to Corinth. (Acts 18:1-18, I Corinthians 1:14-16; 9:6-15; 16:15, II Corinthians 1:19; 11:6-10, I Thessalonians 1:1; 3:6, II Thessalonians 1:1)

   1. Paul stayed with Aquila and Priscilla in Corinth. (Acts 18:1-3)
      a. They were Jews.
      b. They had left Rome at the command of Claudius (Caesar).

   2. Paul worked as a tentmaker. (Acts 18:3)
      a. Paul sacrificed his rights to receive payment for his work in the church. (I Corinthians 9:6-18)
         1) He had to work for his living.
         2) He had a right to reap material benefits.
         3) He endured everything to remove any obstacle in the way of the gospel.

      b. Paul received no help from the Corinthians. (II Corinthians 11:7-9)
         1) He humbled himself to make them important.
         2) He was paid by other churches (example: Philippi, Philippians 4:15).
         3) He was never a burden.

   3. Paul held discussions (reasoned) in the synagogue: (Acts 18:4)
      a. Every Sabbath
      b. He tried to persuade both Jews and Greeks.

   4. Silas and Timothy arrived from Macedonia. (Acts 18:5)
      a. They helped Paul preach the gospel. (II Corinthians 1:19)
      b. They were with him when he wrote the letters to the Thessalonians:
         1) I Thessalonians 1:1
         2) II Thessalonians 1:1

      c. Paul is able to devote himself exclusively to preaching:
         1) Testifying to the Jews
         2) That Jesus was the Christ

      d. Timothy brought back good news to Paul about the faith and love of the church at Thessalonica. (I Thessalonians 3:6)

5. Paul was opposed by the Jews. (Acts 18:6)
    a. The Jews became abusive.
    b. Paul protested.
       1) He shook off the dust from his clothes. (See Matthew 10:14-15)
       2) He absolved himself of blame for their fate. ("Your blood be on your own heads, I am clear of responsibility.")
    c. Paul announced that from now on he would go to the Gentiles.

6. Paul moved in with Titius Justus. (Acts 18:7)
    a. He was a Gentile.
    b. He worshiped God.
    c. He lived next to the synagogue.

7. Many Corinthians heard, believed, and were baptized. (Acts 18:8)
    a. Crispus, the ruler of the synagogue and his family
    b. Gaius (I Corinthians 1:14)
    c. The household of Stephanas (I Corinthians 1:16, 16:15)

8. Paul had another vision. (Acts 18:9-11)
    a. The Lord spoke to him, saying:
       1) Don't be afraid.
       2) Keep speaking.
       3) Don't give up.
       4) I am with you.
       5) No one will be able to harm you.
       6) There are many of my people in this city.

    b. Paul stayed for one and a half years, teaching the people the Word of God.

9. Paul went before Gallio. (Acts 18:12-17)
    a. Gallio was the Roman Governor (Proconsul) of Achaia (the province in which Corinth was located).
    b. The Jews attacked Paul.
       1) They took him to court.
       2) They accused him of trying to persuade people to worship God in an unlawful way.

    c. Gallio would not judge the matter.
       1) He said no evil crime or wrong was done.
       2) He said it was an argument about words, names, and the Jewish Law.
       3) He said that they must settle the matter themselves.
       4) He ejected the Jews and threw the case out

    d. The crowd then beat up Sosthenes in front of the court.
       1) He was the synagogue leader.
       2) Gallio was not concerned about the beating.

e. Note: It is possible that Sosthenes was Crispus' replacement, and that he was beaten by the Greek onlookers. He may have become a Christian later. (I Corinthians 1:1)

10. Paul returned to Antioch. (Acts 18:18-23)
   a. Paul stayed on with the believers in Corinth for many days.
   b. He sailed from Cenchrea (near Corinth).
      1) He was with Priscilla and Aquila.
      2) They sailed for Syria.

   c. Paul had his head shaved because of a vow he had taken (a Jewish custom done after a vow had been fulfilled).

   d. Paul's team arrived in Ephesus.
      1) Paul left Priscilla and Aquila.
      2) Paul went to the synagogue and held discussions (reasoned) with the Jews.
      3) The people wanted him to stay.
         a) Paul declined.
         b) He said he would return if it was God's will.
         c) He sailed from Ephesus.

   e. Paul arrived in Caesarea.
   f. Paul went up and greeted the church ("went up" may mean he went to Jerusalem).
   g. Paul went to Antioch.
      1) He spent some time there.
      2) He left Antioch.
      3) He went through regions of Galatia and Phrygia, strengthening all the disciples.

Lesson Four
Study Questions

1. What had Paul and Barnabas planned to do?

2. Why did they separate?

3. Why did Paul not want to take Mark?

4. Who did Paul choose to go with him?

5. Where did they go?

6. What did they do?

7. Where was Timothy from?

8. What kind of reputation did Timothy have?

9. Why did Paul circumcise Timothy?

10. What were they delivering to the believers?

11. Why didn't they go into the province of Asia?

12. What happened at the border of Mysia?

13. Where did Paul's team go from there?

14. What did Paul see in his vision?

15. What did Paul's team decide to do next?

16. To what city did they go?

17. Why did they go to the riverside on the Sabbath?

18. What did Lydia do for a living?

19. Why did Lydia respond to Paul's message?

20. How do you suppose anyone responds to the gospel?

21. What did Lydia do after she heard Paul?

22. Who were in Philippi with Paul?

23. How do we know Luke was with him?

24. How did the slave girl possessed by an evil spirit benefit her owners?

25. What did the spirit in her say about Paul and his team?

26. Do demons (evil spirits) believe in God? (See James 2:19)

27. What did Paul do about the girl?

28. Why were her owners angry?

29. With what did the owners charge Paul and Silas?

30. Were these charges true?

31. Whose side did the crowd take?

32. Do crowds usually make wise decisions?

33. Are crowds usually swayed by instigators?

34. What does this say about mob justice?

35. What happened next to Paul and Silas?

36. What did they do in prison?

37. How should we respond when we suffer for Christ? (Read I Peter 4:12-16)

38. What caused Paul and Silas to be freed?

39. Why was the jailer about to kill himself?

40. What question did he ask Paul and Silas?

41. What was their answer to his question?

42. How did the jailer and his family respond to the Word of the Lord?

43. Why did they have joy?

44. Why were the officials afraid?

45. What did they do?

46. Before they left Philippi what did Paul and Silas do?

47. Where did Paul preach first in Thessalonica?

48. Who set the city in an uproar?

49. How, according to the Jews, were Paul and Silas breaking the law of Caesar?

50. In what ways was Paul an example to the Thessalonians?

51. What is Paul's rule about work? (II Thessalonians 3:10)

52. Does this rule apply to pastors and church leaders? Why?

53. Paul says he is judged worthy to be entrusted with the gospel. How have some people proven that they are not?

54. Why does Paul say he tries to please God?

55. How did Paul show that he did not try to please man?

56. If we always try to please God, will we always please men as well? Why?

57. What made Paul ready to share his life with the Thessalonian believers?

58. What does this mean for us?

59. Whose example does Paul say the Thessalonians followed?

60. What did the Thessalonians do with the faith?

61. How can we be a good example?

62. Why did Paul and Silas go to Berea at night?

63. What kind of people did they find in the synagogue there?

64. What good example did the Bereans set?

65. Who tried to spoil Paul's ministry in Berea?

66. Where did Paul go next?

67. What upset Paul in Athens?

68. In what two places did Paul have discussions?

69. Why did some people think he was talking about foreign gods?

70. What was the name of Athens' city council?

71. Who did Paul say was the "unknown God"?

72. According to Paul, what does God need from men?

73. According to Paul, how are we related to God?

74. What is God now commanding all men to do?

75. How has God proven that He has chosen Jesus?

76. In what three ways did people respond to Paul's message in Athens?

77. In what ways do you think people respond to our message about Christ today?

78. With whom did Paul stay in Corinth?

79. What sort of work did Paul do there?

80. Why did Paul work with his hands in Corinth?

81. From where did Paul write the letters to the Thessalonians?

82. How did Paul react when the Jews rejected him?

83. What did he say he would do from then on?

84. Where did Titius Justus live?

85. Name three people or families from Corinth who were baptized.

86. What instructions did the Lord give to Paul in his vision?

87. Why do you suppose the Lord told Paul all this?

88. How do these instructions relate to us today?

89. How long did Paul stay in Corinth?

90. How did Gallio respond to the Jews' charges against Paul?

91. When the crowd beat up Sosthenes, what did Gallio do?

92. Who left Corinth with Paul?

93. Why did Paul have his head shaved?

94. Where did Paul leave Aquila and Priscilla?

95. What did Paul say to the people who wanted him to stay at Ephesus?

96. What did Paul do after arriving in Caesarea?

97. Where did he go from there?

98. What did he do in the regions of Galatia and Phrygia?

Lesson Five
V. PAUL'S THIRD MISSIONARY JOURNEY (54-58 A.D.) (Acts 18:22-21:16)

A. Paul Ministers to Various Churches

   1. Paul Revisited the Churches of Galatia and Phrygia. (Acts 18:22-23)
      a. He traveled from place to place.
      b. He strengthened all the disciples.

   2. Apollos Visited Ephesus and Achaia. (Acts 18:24-28)
      a. Apollos was a Jew.
      b. He was born in Alexandria (Egypt).
      c. He was educated.
         1) He was an eloquent speaker.
         2) He had a thorough knowledge of the scriptures.
         3) He had been instructed in the way of the Lord.

   3. Apollos spoke with great fervor and taught about Jesus.
      a. He knew the correct facts about Jesus.
      b. He knew only the baptism of John (the baptism of repentance).

   4. Apollos spoke boldly in the synagogue.
      a. Aquila and Priscilla heard him.
      b. They took him home.
      c. They explained to him more adequately the way of God.

   5. Apollos decided to go to Achaia (Corinth).
      a. The believers helped by sending letters to Achaia.
      b. They asked the Corinthians to welcome him.
      c. He was a great help at Corinth.
         1) He helped new believers.
         2) He refuted the Jews in public debate by proving from scripture that Jesus was the Christ.

B. Paul Went to Ephesus. (Acts 19:1-41)

   1. Paul arrived in Ephesus.
   2. He found twelve disciples. (Acts 19:1-7)
      a. He asked, "Did you receive the Holy Spirit when you believed?"
      b. They had not even heard of the Holy Spirit.
      c. Paul asked what kind of baptism they had received.

d. They answered that they had received John's baptism.
  1) Paul said John's baptism was for repentance.
  2) He said that John had told the people of Israel to believe in Jesus who was to come after him.

e. They were baptized into the name of the Lord Jesus.
  1) Paul placed hands on them.
  2) The Holy Spirit came upon them.
  3) They spoke in tongues.
  4) They prophesied.

3. Paul spoke in the synagogue. (Acts 19:8-10)
  a. He spoke boldly for three months.
  b. He argued persuasively with the people.
    1) He tried to convince the people about the Kingdom of God.
    2) Some would not believe and maligned the way of the Lord.

  c. Paul left with the disciples.
  d. Paul had discussions every day:
    1) At the lecture hall of Tyrannus
    2) For two years

  e. Everyone in the province of Asia, whether Greeks or Jews, heard the word of the Lord.

4. Extraordinary miracles were happening. (Acts 19:11-12)
  a. God did them through Paul.
  b. Items Paul used (aprons and handkerchiefs) were taken to the sick, with wonderful results.
    1) Their diseases were driven away.
    2) Evil spirits went out of them.

5. The Jewish exorcists were defeated. (Acts 19:13-16)
  a. Some Jews who cast out demons tried to use the name of the Lord Jesus.
    1) They said to the spirits, "In the name of Jesus, whom Paul preaches, I command you to come out."
    2) These Jews were the seven sons of Sceva, a chief priest.

  b. The evil spirit replied, "Jesus I know, and I know about Paul, but who are you?"
  c. The man with the spirit attacked them with violence.
    1) He overpowered them all.
    2) He chased them away with a beating, leaving them wounded and naked.

6. The fear of the Lord came to the Ephesians. (Acts 19:17-20)
  a. Jews and Gentiles heard about the exorcists.
    1) They were seized with fear.
    2) The name of the Lord Jesus was held in high honor.

b. Many believers confessed their evil deeds in public.

c. Many sorcerers burned their valuable scrolls in public.

d. In this powerful way the word of the Lord kept spreading widely and growing in power.

7. Paul planned his travels. (Acts 19:21, I Corinthians 16:3-7, Romans 15:22-29)

  a. He decided to travel through:

    1) Macedonia

    2) Achaia

  b. He wanted to spend some time in Jerusalem.

  c. Finally, Paul wanted to see Rome.

  d. Paul planned to come to Corinth to collect money for Jerusalem and take it there. (I Corinthians 16:3-4)

  e. He planned to go to Macedonia first, then spend the winter with the Corinthians. (I Corinthians 16:5-7)

  f. He told the Romans that when he was finished taking the offering to Jerusalem, he would visit them on the way to Spain. (Romans 15:22-28)

8. Timothy and Erastus were sent to Macedonia, then Timothy on to Corinth, while Paul stayed in Ephesus. (Acts 19:22, I Corinthians 4:17; 16:8; 16:10-11)

  a. Paul sent Timothy to the Corinthians. He called Timothy:

    1) His beloved son

    2) Faithful in the Lord

    3) To remind them of Paul's teaching

  b. Paul asked them to welcome Timothy:

    1) Because he was working for the Lord.

    2) He deserved acceptance.

    3) He should receive help to continue his trip.

    4) Paul was expecting him back with the brothers.

  c. Paul said he would stay in Ephesus until the day of Pentecost. (I Corinthians 16:8)

  d. Note: It is believed that Paul wrote I Corinthians about this time from Ephesus.

9. Paul sent Titus to Corinth. (II Corinthians 12:17-18; 7:13-15; 8:6)

  a. He sent Titus with another Christian brother. (II Corinthians 12:17-18)

  b. Titus was well-received there. (II Corinthians 7:13-15)

  c. Paul urged Titus to continue working with them. (II Corinthians 8:6)

10. Demetrius caused trouble for Paul. (Acts 19:23-41)

  a. Demetrius, the silversmith, brought all the idol makers together.

    1) He told them their prosperity comes from making idols (silver shrines).

    2) He told them Paul was saying man-made idols are not gods at all.

3) Paul had convinced many in Ephesus and all over the province of Asia.
4) This presented danger to them, because:
   a) The business would get a bad name.
   b) The main goddess of Ephesus, Artemis, would lose her "divine majesty."

b. The crowd became furious.
1) They shouted, "Great is Artemis of the Ephesians."
2) The uproar spread throughout the whole city.

c. The mob grabbed two of Paul's companions:
1) Gaius
2) Aristarchus
3) They were:
   a) Macedonians
   b) Travelers with Paul

4) The mob rushed them to the theatre.
5) The disciples would not let Paul go before the crowd.
6) Even some of the authorities who were Paul's friends begged him not to show himself there.

d. The meeting turned into an uproar.
1) Confusion reigned.
2) Most people didn't know what was going on.
3) Some thought Alexander was responsible because the Jews made him go to the front.
   a) He tried to talk to the crowd.
   b) They saw he was a Jew and wouldn't listen.
   c) They shouted, "Great is Artemis of the Ephesians" for two hours.

e. The city clerk calmed the crowd.
1) He told them that everyone knew Ephesus was the keeper of the temple of Artemis.
2) He said that they must calm down and not do anything rash.
3) He said that the men they had arrested had not robbed temples or blasphemed Artemis.
4) He said that Demetrius and his workers could bring charges in court if they had a grievance.
5) He said that everything must be settled in a legal assembly of citizens:
   a) Otherwise, they were rioting.
   b) There was no reason for the uproar.

6) He dismissed the meeting.

11. There are other details of Paul's stay in Ephesus. (Acts 20:17-35, I Corinthians 1:1; 4:11-12; 15:30-32; 16:15-19, II Corinthians 1:8-11)
a. Paul mentioned his companions in Ephesus: (I Corinthians 1:1; 16:15-19)
1) Sosthenes
2) Sephanas

3) Fortunatus
4) Achaicus
5) Aquila and Priscilla

(Note: These are in addition to others already mentioned.)

b. Paul mentioned his sufferings in Ephesus.
  1) He said that he had served the Lord: (Acts 20:17-19)
    a) With all humility
    b) With many tears
    c) Endured hard times because of the Jews

  2) He said that he had faced death every day and fought wild beasts at Ephesus.
    (I Corinthians 15:30-32)

  3) The burdens laid on him were great: (II Corinthians 1:8-11)
    a) He gave up the hope of staying alive.
    b) He said the death sentence had been passed on him.
    c) He said God saved him (and his companions) from the terrible dangers of death.

c. Paul recalled his teaching to the Ephesians. (Acts 20:20-32)
  1) He held back nothing that would be of help.
  2) He gave solemn warning to all:
    a) To repent
    b) To believe in our Lord Jesus

  3) He was obeying the Holy Spirit.
    a) He was returning to Jerusalem.
    b) He was not sure what awaited him.
    c) He knew that prison and trouble were in his future.

  4) He considered his own life to be nothing.
  5) He wanted to complete his mission to declare the gospel of the grace of God.
  6) He had preached the Kingdom of God among them.
    a) If any were lost, it was not his fault.
    b) He held back nothing.

  7) He told elders to watch over themselves and their flock:
    a) To be shepherds
    b) Because wolves would come
    c) Men from their own group would lie and mislead the believers.

8) He commended them to the care of God and the message of grace:
    a) Which is able to build you up
    b) Which is able to give you the blessings God has for all His people

    d. Paul recalled his manual labor. (Acts 20:33-35, I Corinthians 4:11-12)
      1) He didn't want anyone's belongings.
      2) He worked with his own hands to provide for himself and his companions.
      3) He went hungry and thirsty, without clothes or a home.
      4) He worked hard as an example:
        a) In helping the weak
        b) In remembering the words of Jesus that it is more blessed to give than to receive.

C. Paul Went to Macedonia. (Acts 20:1-3, II Corinthians 1:1; 2:12-13; 7:5-7; 7:13-16; 8:1-18; 8:16-24; 9:1-5)

  1. Paul left Ephesus.
    a. He headed for Macedonia.
    b. He stopped at Troas: (II Corinthians 2:12-13)
      1) To preach the gospel
      2) He had no rest, and did not find Titus.
      3) He left for Macedonia.

  2. Timothy joined Paul. (II Corinthians 1:1) (Remember, Paul sent Timothy to Macedonia from Ephesus, and II Corinthians was written from Macedonia.)

  3. Titus brought them good news from Corinth. (II Corinthians 7:5-7; 13-16)
    a. They had no rest.
    b. There were troubles everywhere:
      1) Quarrels
      2) Fears

    c. Titus' coming comforted them.
    d. Titus gave a good report from Corinth.

  4. Paul preached throughout Macedonia.
    a. He encouraged the people with many messages. (Acts 20:2)
    b. The church there was tested by troubles. (II Corinthians 8:2)
    c. The church was generous, although poor. (II Corinthians 8:2-5)
      1) They gave more than they could afford.
      2) They begged for the privilege of giving.
      3) They gave themselves to the Lord and to Paul.

  5. Titus returned to Corinth. (II Corinthians 8:6-8; 16-24; 9:1-5)
    a. He was sent to continue the work there.
    b. He was sent along with other respected brothers to collect an offering from the church at Corinth.

c. The group was sent ahead of Paul to collect the gift for the "saints" (probably the church in Jerusalem - I Corinthians 16:1-3).

d. Titus took with him the second letter to the Corinthians.

D. Paul Went to Greece. (Acts 20:2-3, Romans 16:1-2; 21-23)

1. He stayed in Corinth for three months.
2. He changed his plan to leave for Syria.
   a. He went back through Macedonia.
   b. He was avoiding a plot by the Jews against him.

3. He wrote Romans before leaving Corinth.
4. Paul's companions in Corinth included:
   a. Phoebe (Romans 16:1-2)
      1) She was called "our sister."
      2) She served the church at Cenchrea (near Corinth) (probably a deaconess).
      3) Paul instructs the church to receive her (she was probably bringing Paul's letter to the Romans from Corinth).
      4) He told them to help her.
      5) He said she was a good friend to many.

   b. Timothy (Romans 16:21)
      1) He was Paul's fellow worker.
      2) He sent his greetings.

   c. Lucius (probably of Cyrene, Acts 13:1)
   d. Jason (Paul's host at Thessalonica, Acts 17:1-7)
   e. Sopater (the Berean, Acts 20:4)
   f. Tertius (Paul's secretary who was taking dictation for the letter to the Romans)
   g. Gaius (Paul's host, baptized by Paul, I Corinthians 1:14)
   h. Erastus (City Treasurer of Corinth)
   i. Quartus

E. Paul Journeyed to Jerusalem. (Acts 20:1-38, Acts 21:1-16, Romans 15:25-29)

1. Paul was going to Jerusalem to serve God's people. (Romans 15:25-29)
   a. He was going to deliver an offering from the churches at Macedonia and Achaia.
   b. He planned to visit the Romans on the way to Spain after delivering the offering.

2. Paul sailed from Philippi to Troas. (Acts 20:3-12)
   a. He changed plans because of the Jewish plot against him.

b. Some brothers went ahead to Troas, including:
  1) Sopater of Berea
  2) Aristarchus and Secundus of Thessalonica
  3) Gaius of Derbe
  4) Timothy (Paul's assistant)
  5) Tychicus and Trophimus of Asia

c. Luke seemed to have rejoined Paul here. (Note "we" used again for the first time since Acts 16:17.)
d. The trip took five days.
e. At Troas Paul spent a week ministering.
f. Eutychus was raised up from death.
  1) Paul preached until midnight.
  2) Eutychus fell asleep in the window.
  3) Eutychus fell from the third story.
  4) The believers found him dead.
  5) Paul embraced him and pronounced that Eutychus was alive.
  6) Eutychus got up and ate.

g. Paul continued to share until dawn.
h. Everyone was greatly comforted by the miracle.

3. Paul went on to Miletus. (Acts 20:13-38)
  a. Paul's companions went ahead by ship.
    1) Paul proceeded by land.
    2) Paul met the others at Assos.
    3) He took the ship to:
      a) Mitylene
      b) Kios
      c) Samos
      d) Miletus

    4) Paul decided to sail past Ephesus.
      a) He was trying to save time.
      b) He wanted to arrive in Jerusalem before the day of Pentecost.

  b. Paul addressed the Ephesian elders at Miletus. (Acts 20:17-38) (This is mentioned earlier in the lesson.)
  1) He called the elders of the church.
  2) He recounted his previous time with them.
    a) He had done his work as God's servant:
      (1) With great humility
      (2) With many tears
      (3) Severely tested
      (4) In spite of Jewish plots

b) He did not hold back anything as he preached, and taught in public and
   from house to house.
  (1) He gave solemn warning to repent from sin and to have faith in the Lord Jesus.
  (2) He warned Jews and Gentiles alike.

 c) He was now obeying (compelled by) the Holy Spirit:
  (1) Returning to Jerusalem
  (2) Knowing troubles awaited him

 d) He considered his own life to be worth nothing to him.
  (1) He wanted only to complete his mission.
  (2) He wanted to finish the task the Lord Jesus had given him to do.
  (3) He wanted to testify to the gospel of God's grace.

 e) He had preached the Kingdom of God among them.
 f) He did not expect to be seen by them again.
 g) He could not be held responsible if any of them should be lost
    (innocent of the blood of all men).
 h) He had not held back proclaiming the whole will of God.

3) The last instructions from Paul were:
  a) To keep watch:
   (1) Over themselves
   (2) Over all the flock the Holy Spirit had placed in their care

  b) To be shepherds of the church of God which God bought with His own blood

  c) To be warned that:
   (1) "Savage wolves" would come among them not sparing the flock
   (2) Some of their own men would tell lies and lead the believers away
  d) To be on guard and remember that he had taught them all for three years night and day
     with many tears

  e) To be committed to God:
   (1) To His care
   (2) To the word of His grace:
      (a) Able to build them up
      (b) Able to give them an inheritance among all who are sanctified (set apart for
          a holy purpose)

4) Paul gave his final testimony to the Ephesian elders.
   a) Paul had not coveted anyone's possessions.
   b) Paul had worked to meet his own needs and those of his companions.
     (1) He was demonstrating that we must help the weak by hard work.
     (2) He was remembering that Jesus said, "It is more blessed to give than to receive."

5) Paul bid his final farewell to the elders.
   a) They prayed together.
   b) They bid good-bye with hugs and kisses.
   c) They cried because they wouldn't see him again.
   d) They accompanied Paul to the ship.

4. Paul and his group sailed on to Tyre. (Acts 21:1-6)
   a. They sailed to Cos, Rhodes, and to Patara.
   b. They found a ship headed to Phoenicia and proceeded by Cyprus to Syria and Tyre.
   c. At Tyre, Paul and his group stayed with disciples for a week.
     1) Paul was urged by the disciples through the Spirit not to go to Jerusalem.
     2) They left and went on their way anyway.
     3) All the disciples went with them to the beach to pray with Paul and his group.
     4) Paul and his group continued their voyage to Jerusalem.

5. Paul completed his voyage to Jerusalem. (Acts 21:7-16)
   a. Paul's group arrived at Ptolemais.
     1) They greeted the brothers.
     2) They stayed for a day.

   b. They arrived in Caesarea the next day.
     1) They stayed with Philip, the evangelist.
       a) He was one of the deacons chosen in Jerusalem ("the Seven").
       b) He had four unmarried daughters who prophesied.

     2) Agabus arrived.
       a) He was a prophet.
       b) He was from Judea.
       c) He prophesied that Paul would be tied up by the Jews and turned over to the Gentiles at Jerusalem.

     3) Paul's group begged him not to go.
     4) Paul insisted that he was ready to die for the sake of the Lord Jesus.
     5) The group gave up saying, "The Lord's will be done."

   c. Paul's group left for Jerusalem.
     1) Some disciples from Caesarea also went.
     2) They took Paul to stay with an early disciple from Cyprus named Mnason.

Lesson Five
Study Questions

1.   What were some of Apollos' qualifications?

2.   What limitation did he have?

3.   Who helped Apollos learn more?

4.   What did Apollos decide to do?

5.   How did the believers in Ephesus help him?

6.   What are two ways Apollos was a help in Corinth?

7.   What was the problem with the twelve disciples?

8.   What sort of baptism is John's, according to Paul?

9.   When they were baptized in the name of the Lord, what happened?

10.   How long did Paul speak at the synagogue?

11.   Of what did he try to convince people there?

12.   Why did he leave with believers?

13. Where did he continue his discussions?

14. How long did he continue there?

15. How was God's power shown with Paul?

16. Did the evil spirits obey the Jews?

17. What did they do to the Jews?

18. Does one need to be a Christian to make spiritual warfare? Why?

19. When the fear of the Lord came to the Ephesians, what happened?

20. Why is it important to repent in public?

21. Why did Paul plan to return to Jerusalem?

22. Whom did Paul send to Macedonia?

23. Where did Timothy go next?

24. Why did Paul call Timothy his beloved son?

25. Who else was sent to Corinth?

26. Why did Demetrius think Paul was a danger?

27. Who did the crowd grab?

28. Who protected Paul?

29. Why was there so much confusion?

30. Do crowds make good juries? Why, or why not?

31. Why wouldn't the crowd listen to Alexander?

32. Who calmed the crowd?

33. What was his opinion?

34. Was ministry easy for Paul in Ephesus? What were some of his problems?

35. What was Paul's solemn warning to the Ephesians?

36. What did he tell the elders to do?

37. What two things did he commend the Ephesians to?

38. What attitude did Paul have about being required to work with his hands?

39. Should pastors or evangelists work with their hands? Why, or why not?

40. Why did Paul stop at Troas on the way to Macedonia?

41. Who joined Paul in Macedonia?

42. From where was Titus coming?

43. What impressed Paul about the church in Macedonia?

44. Can a church be too poor to contribute to others?

45. For what reasons did Titus return to Corinth?

46. Which letter did Paul write during his stay in Corinth?

47. Which person did Paul refer to as "our sister" who worked with him at Corinth?

48. Why was Erastus an important man in Corinth?

49. Should Christians avoid public office?

50. What was the main reason for Paul's return to Jerusalem?

51. Why do we think Luke joined Paul at Phillipi on the way to Troas?

52. What miracle happened to Eutychus at Troas?

53. Why did Paul skip Ephesus on his return to Jerusalem?

54. Where did he meet the elders from Ephesus?

55. What had been his solemn warning at Ephesus?

56. Is it possible to believe in Jesus without recognizing his Lordship?

57. What did Paul most want to do?

58. What should we most want to do?

59. What did Paul preach among the Ephesians?

60. What did he instruct the elders to be?

61. According to Paul the message of God's grace is able to do two things. What are they?

62. How did Paul say he met his and his companions' needs?

63. Should pastors and Christian workers expect churches to provide for them?

64. Why were the elders so sad?

65. At Tyre the believers had a word by the power of the Holy Spirit. What was it?

66. Why did Paul go anyway?

67. What was interesting about Philip the evangelist's daughters?

68. Is it scriptural for women to exercise gift ministries?

69. What prophecy did Agabus give Paul?

70. What response did Paul give when the believers at Caesarea begged him not to go to Jerusalem?

Lesson Six

VI. PAUL'S FIFTH VISIT TO JERUSALEM AND IMPRISONMENT AT CAESAREA (Acts 21:17-26:32)

Dates: 58-60 A.D.

A. Paul's Vow (Acts 21:17-26)

1. Paul arrived in Jerusalem.
   a. He was received warmly by the brothers.
   b. Paul and his company went to see James.
      1) All the elders were present.
      2) Paul greeted them and reported in detail what God had done among the Gentiles through his ministry.
      3) The elders praised God.

   c. The elders explained to Paul the misunderstanding about his teaching among the Jews.
      1) The believing Jews were zealous for the Law.
      2) The believing Jews had been told that Paul was teaching Jews to turn from the Law of Moses:
         a) Not to circumcise
         b) Not to live according to Jewish customs

      3) The elders were concerned about the Jews' reaction to Paul's coming.

2. Paul was instructed by the Jerusalem elders to make a vow.
   a. The elders told him to join with four others who had made a vow:
      1) To be purified with them
      2) To pay their expenses so their heads could be shaved

   b. The result would be that the bad report concerning Paul would be disproved.
   c. Paul would be recognized as one who keeps the Law.
   d. The elders reminded Paul of their decision concerning Gentile believers:
      1) They should abstain from food sacrificed to idols.
      2) They should abstain from blood.
      3) They should abstain from meat from strangled animals.
      4) They should abstain from sexual immorality.

3. Paul followed the elders' instructions.
   a. He purified himself with the four men.
   b. He went to the temple:
      1) To give notice of the date when the days of purification would end
      2) To give notice when the offering would be made for each of them

B. Paul Was Arrested at the Temple. (Acts 21:27-22:29)

1. Paul was seized by some Jews from Asia when they saw him in the temple.
   a. They stirred up the whole crowd.
      1) They accused Paul of teaching against the Jews, the Law, and the temple.
      2) They accused Paul of defiling the temple by bringing a Greek (Trophimus) into it (an assumption).

   b. The whole city became aroused.
      1) The people came running.
      2) They seized Paul.
         a) They dragged him from the temple.
         b) They tried to kill him.

   c. The news reached the Roman commander about the uproar.
      1) He took officers and soldiers and ran to the crowd.
      2) The crowd stopped beating Paul when they saw the soldiers.

   d. The commander arrested Paul.
      1) He bound him with two chains.
      2) He asked who he was and what he had done.

   e. The uproar caused much confusion.
      1) Some in the crowd shouted one thing, others another.
      2) The commander could not get at the truth.
      3) He had Paul taken to the barracks.
         a) The violence of the mob was great
         b) Paul had to be carried by the soldiers.
         c) The crowd continued to shout at Paul.

2. Paul addressed the crowd.
   a. Paul asked to speak to the commander.
      1) The commander was surprised because:
         a) Paul spoke Greek.
         b) The commander thought Paul was an Egyptian rebel.

      2) Paul told him he was a Jew and a citizen of Tarsus.
      3) Paul asked if he could speak to the people.
      4) The commander agreed to let Paul speak.

   b. Paul spoke to the crowd.
      1) He stood on the steps of the barracks.
      2) He quieted the crowd.
      3) He spoke to them in Aramaic.

4) Paul explained his background:
  a) A Jew
  b) Born in Tarsus, raised in Jerusalem
  c) Trained in the Law by Gamaliel
  d) Zealous for God
  e) Persecuted the followers of the Way:
    (1) To their death
    (2) Arresting men and women
    (3) Throwing them in prison
    (4) Obtained letters to arrest believers in Damascus and bring them to Jerusalem for punishment

5) Paul recounted his Damascus road experience.
  a) He saw the bright light from heaven.
  b) He heard the voice saying, "Saul, Saul, why do you persecute Me?"
  c) Only Paul understood the voice.
  d) Paul asked what to do.
  e) The Lord instructed Paul.
    (1) He told him to go to Damascus.
    (2) He said he would be given assignments.
    (3) Paul was blinded temporarily.

  f) Paul was led by his companions to Damascus.
  g) Ananias came to see Paul.
    (1) Ananias was a devout observer of the Law.
    (2) He was highly respected by all the Jews.
    (3) He restored Paul's sight by command.

  h) Ananias commissioned Paul.
    (1) He said Paul was chosen by God.
    (2) He said Paul was to know God's will, see the Righteous One, and hear His words.
    (3) He said Paul would be His witness to all men.
    (4) He told Paul to be baptized to wash his sins away, and to call on the name of Jesus.

  i) Paul had a vision at the temple in Jerusalem.
    (1) The Lord appeared to Paul in a trance.
    (2) He told him to leave Jerusalem immediately.
    (3) He warned that his testimony would be rejected.
    (4) Paul confessed to persecuting the believers and approving the murder of Stephen.
    (5) The Lord told Paul to "Go"; he would be sent to the Gentiles.

3. Paul declared his Roman citizenship.
  a. The crowd reacted to Paul's speech.
    1) They shouted that he should be killed.
    2) They threw off their cloaks and dust into the air.

  b. The commander ordered Paul to be taken into the barracks:
    1) To be flogged (beaten)
    2) To be questioned to find out what was causing the problem

  c. Paul asked the centurion if it was legal to flog a Roman citizen.
    1) He reported Paul's citizenship to the commander.
    2) The commander confirmed the fact with Paul.
      a) He said he had to pay a large price for his citizenship.
      b) Paul said he was born a citizen.

    3) The proceedings stopped.
      a) The questioners withdrew.
      b) The commander was alarmed that he had put a Roman citizen in chains.

C. Paul Appeared Before the Sanhedrin. (Acts 22:30-23:11)

1. The commander decided to determine the nature of the Jews' accusations against Paul.
  a. He released Paul.
  b. He ordered the chief priests and Sanhedrin to assemble.
  c. He brought Paul before them.

2. Paul addressed the Sanhedrin.
  a. He said he had fulfilled his duty to God in good conscience.
  b. The high priest, Ananias, had Paul struck in the mouth.
    1) Paul reacted:
      a) He warned that God would strike Ananias.
      b) He called him a white-washed stone.
      c) He pointed out that Ananias was judging by the Law while breaking it himself.

    2) Paul apologized.
      a) He was told Ananias was the high priest.
      b) Paul stated he didn't realize that fact.
      c) Paul confirmed that one should not speak evil about the ruler of the people.

  c. Paul created a controversy.
    1) He knew some of the Sanhedrin were Sadducees and some were Pharisees.
      a) He stated he was a Pharisee.
      b) He stated that the whole issue was over his hope in the resurrection of the dead.

2) A dispute broke out.
  a) The Sadducees didn't believe in the resurrection while the Pharisees did.
  b) There was a great uproar.
  c) Some of the teachers of the Pharisees began to argue on behalf of Paul.
  d) The dispute became violent.

3) The commander ordered Paul removed to the barracks.
  a) He feared Paul would be harmed.
  b) He removed Paul by force with his troops.

3. The Lord appeared to Paul.
  a. He stood near him the following night.
  b. He spoke to him:
    1) "Take courage."
    2) "As you have testified about me in Jerusalem, so you must also testify in Rome."

D. The Jews Conspired Against Paul. (Acts 23:12-30)

1. An oath was taken by the Jews.
  a. They bound themselves not to eat or drink until they killed Paul.
    1) More than forty men were involved.
    2) They informed the chief priests and elders.

  b. The Jews and the Sanhedrin wanted to trick the Roman commander into bringing Paul to them in order that he might be ambushed.

2. The plot was exposed.
  a. Paul's nephew heard of the plot.
  b. He informed Paul.
  c. He informed the Roman commander.
    1) The commander dismissed Paul's nephew.
    2) He cautioned him not to tell anyone that he had reported the plot.

3. Paul was transferred to Caesarea.
  a. The commander prepared to move Paul to Caesarea to Governor Felix.
    1) He ordered an armed escort for Paul, which included:
      a) 200 soldiers
      b) 70 horsemen
      c) 200 spearmen

    2) He ordered a transfer for that evening.
    3) He provided horses for Paul.

b. The commander sent a letter with Paul to Felix.
   1) He said he had rescued Paul from the Jews because he was a Roman citizen.
   2) He said the Sanhedrin could give no charge that deserve punishment.
   3) He said that a plot against Paul caused him to send Paul to Felix immediately.
   4) He said that he ordered Paul's accusers to present their case before Felix.

E. Paul Was Tried Before Felix. (Acts 23:31-24:27)

1. Paul was moved to Caesarea.
   a. The soldiers escorted Paul to Antipatris.
   b. The next day the cavalry took Paul on to Caesarea.
   c. The cavalry delivered Paul and the letter to Governor Felix.
   d. The Governor read the letter.
      1) He found that Paul was from the province of Cilicia.
      2) He agreed to hear Paul's case.
      3) He ordered Paul to be kept under guard at Herod's palace.

2. The Jews presented their case.
   a. Ananias, the high priest, arrived with his company, including:
      1) Some elders
      2) Tertullus, the lawyer

   b. Tertullus presented his case.
      1) He expressed appreciation to Felix for:
         a) Peace
         b) Reforms
         c) Hearing the case

      2) He brought charges against Paul, saying:
         a) Paul was a troublemaker.
         b) He was stirring up riots among the Jews.
         c) He was the ringleader of the Nazarene sect.
         d) He tried to desecrate the temple.

      3) The Jews testified to the "truth" of Tertullus' charges.

3. Paul presented his case.
   a. Felix allowed Paul to speak.
   b. Paul defended himself.
      1) He expressed his appreciation to Felix for:
         a) His long term as judge
         b) Allowing him to make his defense

2) Paul recounted the facts.
   a) He was in Jerusalem to worship.
   b) He was not arguing or stirring up controversy.
   c) The charges could not be proved.

3) Paul gave his testimony.
   a) He worshiped the "God of our Fathers."
   b) He was a follower of the "Way."
   c) He believed in the Law and the prophets.
   d) He had hope in the resurrection.
   e) He always strived to keep his conscience clear before God and man.

4) Paul gave additional facts.
   a) He had come to Jerusalem to bring gifts and offerings to the poor.
   b) He was ceremonially clean.
   c) There was no crowd or disturbance.
   d) The Jews from Asia should be bringing the charges.
   e) Those present should state what crime he had committed before the Sanhedrin.
   f) He repeated that resurrection of the dead was the ultimate issue.

c. Felix adjourned the meeting.
  1) He was well acquainted with the "Way."
  2) He told Paul he would decide the case when Lysias (the Roman commander) arrived.
  3) He ordered Paul to be kept under guard with some freedom and company.

d. Felix and his wife, Drusilla, listened to Paul.
  1) Drusilla was a Jewess.
  2) Felix was acquainted with the "Way."
  3) Paul spoke to them about faith in Christ Jesus.
   a) Paul spoke at length on righteousness, self-control, and the judgment.
   b) Felix became afraid.

  4) Felix kept Paul for two years.
   a) He hoped Paul would offer a bribe.
   b) He sent for Paul frequently and talked to him.

  5) Felix was succeeded by Porcius Festus.
   a) Paul was left in prison.
   b) Felix wanted to grant the Jews a favor.

F. Paul Was Tried Before Festus. (Acts 25:1-26:32)
  1. The chief priests and Jewish leaders appealed to Festus to transfer Paul to Jerusalem.
  a. They presented charges against Paul to Festus while he was visiting Jerusalem.
  b. They were preparing to ambush and kill Paul.
  c. Festus invited some of the Jewish leaders to come to Caesarea to press charges against Paul.

2. Festus convened the court in Caesarea.
   a. The Jews from Jerusalem brought many serious charges which they could not prove.
   b. Paul made his defense.
      1) He said he had done nothing wrong:
         a) Against the Jewish Law
         b) Against the temple
         c) Against Caesar

      2) He was unwilling to return to Jerusalem for trial.
         a) Festus wanted to do a favor for the Jews.
         b) Paul stated he was being tried in the right court.
         c) Paul reaffirmed he was innocent of the charges.

   c. Paul appealed to Caesar.
      1) The Jews' charges were not true.
      2) No one had the right to turn him over to the Jews (he was a Roman citizen).
      3) He appealed to Caesar.
      4) Festus agreed to send Paul after conferring with his counsel.

3. Paul appeared before King Agrippa.
   a. King Agrippa and his wife, Bernice, arrived in Caesarea to visit Festus.
      1) Festus discussed Paul's case with Agrippa.
         a) The Jews asked that Paul be condemned.
         b) Festus had insisted upon a fair trial for Paul.
         c) Charges were based on disputes over religion.
         d) Paul refused to go to trial in Jerusalem and appealed to Caesar.

      2) Agrippa, himself, desired to hear Paul.

   b. Paul was presented to Agrippa and Bernice.
      1) Agrippa, Bernice, high ranking officers, and leading men of the city gathered in the
         audience room.
      2) Paul was brought into the room.
      3) Festus explained the case:
         a) The Jews demanded his death.
         b) Paul was not guilty of anything deserving of death.
         c) Paul made an appeal to Caesar.
         d) Festus was looking for something to write to Caesar specifying the charges against Paul.

   c. Agrippa gave permission for Paul to speak.
      1) Paul defended himself.
         a) He expressed appreciation to be heard by Agrippa.
            (1) Agrippa was well acquainted with Jewish customs and controversies.
            (2) Paul asked to be listened to patiently.

b) Paul expressed the nature of his case.
  (1) He was a strict Jew from a child.
  (2) He was a Pharisee.
  (3) His hope in God's promise to "our fathers" was the reason for the Jews' charges.
  (4) He appealed to Agrippa concerning resurrection.

2) Paul recounted his conversion.
  a) He had opposed Jesus of Nazareth.
  (1) He had imprisoned many saints.
  (2) He had cast his vote for their death.
  (3) He had gone from synagogue to synagogue to punish them.
  (4) He had tried to force them to blaspheme.
  (5) He had gone to foreign cities to persecute them.

  b) He had encountered Jesus on the road to Damascus, experiencing:
  (1) The light from heaven
  (2) The voice in Aramaic
  (3) The Lord's instructions to him:
      (a)To be a servant and witness
      (b)To be rescued from Jews and Gentiles
      (c)To be sent:
        [1] To open their eyes
        [2] To turn them from their darkness to light
        [3] To turn them from the power of Satan to God
        [4] To make possible forgiveness of sins and a place among those sanctified by
            faith in Christ

  c) He was obedient to the vision.
    (1) He had preached repentance and turning to God with good deeds:
      (a) In Damascus
      (b) In Jerusalem
      (c) In all Judea
      (d) To the Gentiles

    (2) His preaching was the cause of the wrath of the Jews.
    (3) He testified to all that which Moses and the prophets had foretold concerning Christ.
      (a) Christ would suffer.
      (b) He would be the first to rise from the dead.
      (c) He would proclaim light to His own people.
      (d) He would proclaim light to the Gentiles.

3) Festus interrupted Paul's defense.
   a) He said Paul's great learning had driven him insane.
   b) Paul insisted upon the truth of his testimony.
     (1) He noted Agrippa was familiar with what he was saying.
     (2) He noted that everything he had said was public knowledge.
     (3) He asked Agrippa if he believed in the prophets.
     (4) Agrippa asked if Paul was trying to convert him to Christ.
     (5) Paul affirmed that he wished everyone would become a Christian.

4) Paul's innocence was verified.
   a) All agreed that Paul had done nothing to deserve death.
   b) Agrippa told Festus that Paul could have been set free if he had not appealed to Caesar.

Lesson Six
Study Questions

1. How were Paul and his company received by the brothers in Jerusalem?

2. Who did they go to see?

3. How did the elders in Jerusalem respond to Paul's report about the Gentiles?

4. Why were the believing Jews concerned about Paul's teaching?

5. How do rumors and false reports create misunderstandings and controversies in the Church today?

6. How should pastors respond to second-hand information about others?

7. Why did the Jerusalem elders want Paul to be purified with some other brothers?

8. What were the four "Jewish" restrictions placed on Gentile believers?

9. Are Christians today bound by all of these restrictions? Which one(s)?

10. Did Paul follow the elders' instructions? Did it keep him out of trouble?

11. Who seized Paul in the temple?

12.	With what two things did they charge Paul?

13.	What did the crowd do with Paul?

14.	Why did the crowd stop beating Paul?

15.	What did the Roman commanders do with Paul?

16.	Why was he taken to the Roman barracks?

17.	What did Paul tell the crowd?

18.	Who among Paul's company had heard the Lord's voice?

19.	Who came to see Paul in Damascus?

20.	What sort of a person was he?

21.	What four things did Ananias say to Paul when he commissioned him?

22.	What did the Lord tell Paul to do in his trance?

23. Where did the Lord say He would send Paul?

24. What did the crowd want done to Paul?

25. Why did the commander of the Roman troops become alarmed?

26. Why did the commander call together the Sanhedrin?

27. What did Paul tell the Sanhedrin he had done?

28. What did the high priest, Ananias, do?

29. What charge did Paul make against Ananias?

30. Why did Paul apologize?

31. Why did Paul make it clear that he was a Pharisee?

32. Why did that create a problem in the Sanhedrin?

33. Why did the commander return Paul to the barracks?

34.   Why do you think people get so "worked up" when religious issues are discussed?

35.   What did the Lord tell Paul he must do?

36.   What oath did forty of the "Jews" take?

37.   What did they ask the Sanhedrin to do?

38.   Does murder ever glorify God or His people?

39.   Did the Jews have God's interest in mind or their own?

40.   How can we avoid the same mistake the Jews were making?

41.   How was the plot disclosed?

42.   Where was Paul moved?

43.   Why was he moved at night by so many soldiers?

44.   Why did the commander tell Governor Felix he had rescued Paul?

45.   What did he think of the Sanhedrin's charges?

46. Who came to Caesarea to make a case for the Jews?

47. With what four things did Tertullus charge Paul?

48. Why did Paul say he was in Jerusalem in the first place?

49. According to Paul, he was a follower of what?

50. Whom did he worship?

51. In what did he believe?

52. Why else had he come to Jerusalem?

53. According to Paul, who should have been bringing the charges?

54. What did he maintain was the whole issue?

55.   Was Felix aware of the "Way"?

56.   Who was Drusilla?

57.   What did Paul discuss with Felix and Drusilla?

58.   Why did Felix become afraid?

59.   Why do those things frighten politicians?

60.   Why did Felix keep Paul in prison?

61.   Why did he not release Paul when he was replaced?

62.   Who replaced Felix?

63.   Why did the Jews want Festus to move Paul to Jerusalem?

64.   Why did Festus invite the Jews to Caesarea?

65.   Could they prove their charges?

66.   Was Paul willing to be tried in Jerusalem?

67. Why did no one have a right to turn him over to the Jews?

68. What did Paul finally do to protect himself?

69. What did Festus decide?

70. Who came to visit Festus in Caesarea?

71. According to Festus, the charges against Paul were based on what?

72. What did Agrippa want?

73. What did Festus want from Agrippa?

74. Why was Paul glad to speak to Agrippa?

75. What two things did Paul say the Lord told him to do?

76. He had been sent to the Jews and the Gentiles for what four reasons?

77. What had Paul preached everywhere?

78. According to Paul, what four things had Moses and the prophets foretold about Christ?

79. What did Festus say about Paul

80. What did Paul ask Agrippa?

81. What did Agrippa ask Paul?

82. What was Paul's answer?

83. On what did all agree?

84. Why could Paul not be set free?

85. Do you think God was using all this for His purposes? Why, or why not?

Lesson Seven

VII. PAUL'S JOURNEY TO ROME AND INITIAL CAPTIVITY (Acts 27:1-28:31, Romans 16:3-15, and portions of the "Prison Epistles": Philemon, Colossians, Ephesians and Philippians)

A. Paul Journeyed from Caesarea to Rome. (Acts 27:1-28:16) Date: About 60 A.D.

1. Paul, Aristarchus, and Luke set sail.
   a. Paul and other prisoners were handed over to the centurion, Julius.
   b. The "we" in verse 27:1 indicates Luke was with Paul
   c. Aristarchus, a Macedonian from Thessalonica was with them.

2. The ship went to Crete.
   a. At Sidon Julius allowed Paul to see friends and have his needs met
   b. The ship landed at Myra in Lycia.
   c. The centurion put the party on an Alexandrian ship sailing for Italy.
      1) They had difficulty holding course.
      2) They stopped at Fair Havens in Crete.

   d. Paul warned that the trip would be disastrous.
      1) The centurion listened to the pilot and ship owner instead.
      2) The harbor was unsuitable for wintering.
      3) The majority decided to sail on to Phoenix to winter.

3. The ship was caught by a storm
   a. Hurricane force winds (the Northeaster) drove the ship.
   b. The ship took a violent battering.
      1) They threw the cargo overboard.
      2) They gave up hope of being saved.

   c. Paul encouraged the men.
      1) They had gone a long time without food.
      2) He told them they should have listened to him.
      3) He told them that no one would be lost.
      4) He told them about the angel of God who appeared to him, saying:
      a) "Do not be afraid, Paul."
      b) "You must stand trial before Caesar."
      c) "God has graciously given you the lives of all who sail with you."

      5) He told them to keep up their courage.
      a) He had faith in God's message.
      b) The ship would run aground on an island.

4. The ship ran aground and was destroyed.
   a. After fourteen days the ship was nearing land.
      1) They dropped anchor and prayed for daylight.

2) The sailors tried to desert with the lifeboat.
3) Paul warned the centurion and the soldiers to let the lifeboat fall away.

  b. Paul encouraged the men again.
    1) He urged them to eat.
    2) He assured them of survival.
    3) All 276 men aboard ate and were encouraged.
    4) They threw the grain into the sea.

  c. The men decided to run the ship aground at daylight.
    1) They saw a sandy beach.
    2) They cut loose the anchors and made for the beach.
    3) The ship struck a sandbar and broke into pieces.

  d. Everyone reached land safely.
    1) The soldiers were going to kill the prisoners to prevent escape.
    2) The centurion wanted to save Paul's life.
    3) He stopped the soldiers' plan.
    4) He ordered those who could swim to jump overboard.
    5) The others were able to get to safety on planks and pieces of the ship.

5. Paul stayed in Malta for three months.
  a. The island was called Malta.
    1) The islanders were unusually kind.
    2) They built a fire and welcomed the men.

  b. Paul was bitten by a viper.
    1) The people thought Paul must be a murderer because:
    a) He had escaped the sea.
    b) However, Justice had caught up with him.
    2) Paul shook off the snake with no ill effects.
    3) The people decided Paul must be a god.

  c. Publius welcomed Paul to his home.
    1) He was the chief official of the island.
    2) He entertained Paul and his party for three days.
    3) His father was sick.
    4) Paul healed Publius' father:
    a) After prayer
    b) After laying on of hands

  d. Paul and his company won favor from the islanders.
    1) The rest of the sick on the island were cured when they came to Paul.
    2) They honored Paul's company in many ways.
    3) They furnished Paul's company with needed supplies.

6. Paul arrived in Italy.
   a. Paul's company sailed from Malta on another Alexandrian ship.
      1) He stayed at Syracuse for 3 days.
      2) He reached Puteoli.
         a) He found "brothers" there.
         b) He spent a week at Puteoli.

   b. Paul came to Rome.
      1) The brothers in Rome came to greet Paul.
      2) Paul thanked God and was encouraged at the sight of the brothers.

   c. Paul was allowed to live by himself with a soldier to guard him in Rome.

B. Paul Lived in Captivity. (Acts 28:17-31, Romans 16:3-15) Dates: 61-63 A.D.

   1. The church in Rome (Romans 16:3-15); it included:
      a. Priscilla and Aquila and the church at their house
      b. Epenetus, the first convert from Asia
      c. Mary, who worked hard for them
      d. Andronicus and Junias; they:
         1) Were Paul's relatives
         2) Had been in prison with Paul
         3) Were outstanding among the apostles
         4) Were in Christ before Paul

      e. Ampliatus, whom Paul loved in the Lord
      f. Urbanus and Stachys, fellow worker and dear friend
      g. Apelles, tested and approved in Christ
      h. Aristobulus' household
      i. Herodion, Paul's relative
      j. Narcissus' household
      k. Tryphena and Tryphosa, hard-working women in the Lord
      l. Persis, another hard-working woman
      m. Rufus and his mother (who had been a mother to Paul); perhaps Rufus is son of Simon of
         Cyrene, who carried the cross of Jesus (Mark 15:21)
      n. Others included:
         1) Asyncritus
         2) Phlegon
         3) Hermes
         4) Patrobas
         5) Hermas
         6) The brothers with them
         7) Philologus
         8) Julia
         9) Nereus and his sister

10) Olympas
11) All the saints with them
12) The saints who belong to Caesar's household (Philippians 4:22)

2. Paul met with the Jews in Rome.
  a. He called together the leaders of the Jews.
  b. He explained his situation.
    1) He had done nothing against the Jews or their customs.
    2) He had been arrested and handed over to the Romans.
    3) He had been found innocent by the Romans.
    4) He had appealed to Caesar in self-defense.
    5) He had been bound because of the hope of Israel.

  c. The Jews responded positively.
    1) They had no bad report concerning Paul.
    2) They had heard bad reports concerning this "sect" (Christians).
    3) They wanted to hear Paul's views.

  d. The Jews had an audience with Paul.
    1) Many came.
    2) He spent the whole day with them.
    3) He explained and declared to them the Kingdom of God.
    4) He tried to convince them about Jesus:
     a) From the Law of Moses
     b) From the prophets
    5) They disagreed among themselves.
     a) Some were convinced.
     b) Others would not believe.

  e. Paul made a final statement.
    1) He quoted Isaiah 6:9-10:
     a) Ever hearing, never understanding
     b) Ever seeing, never perceiving
     c) Calloused hearts
     d) Deaf and blind
     e) Otherwise, they would see, hear, and understand and they would turn and be healed by God
    2) He said God's salvation had been sent to the Gentiles who would listen.

  f. Paul preached the Kingdom and taught about the Lord Jesus Christ:
    1) For two years
    2) From his own rented house
    3) Welcoming all who came
    4) Boldly and without hindrance
    [NOTE: Compare this passage with II Timothy 2:9. The different circumstances indicate two separate imprisonments.]

C. Paul's First Roman Imprisonment According to the "Prison Epistles" (Philemon, Colossians, Ephesians, and Philippians)

1. Paul was, indeed, a prisoner.
   a. Philemon 1, 8, 9
   b. Colossians 4:3, 18
   c. Ephesians 3:1; 4:1; 6:18-20
   d. Philippians 1:7; 1:12-14; 1:16

2. Paul expected to be released.
   a. Philemon 22
   b. Philippians 1:23-27; 2:24

3. Paul had companions with him:
   a. Timothy (Paul's "son in the Lord")
      1) Philemon 1
      2) Colossians 1:1
      3) Philippians 1:1; 2:19-23

   b. Epaphra (evangelist who founded the Church at Colossae
      1) Philemon 23
      2) Colossians 1:3-8; 4:12-13

   c. Onesimus (the runaway slave)
      1) Philemon 10-21
      2) Colossians 4:9

   d. Tychicus (bearer of the letter to the Colossians)
      1) Colossians 4:7-9
      2) Ephesians 6:21-22

   e. Others:
      1) Mark (Philemon 24, Colossians 4:10)
      2) Aristarchus (Philemon 24, Colossians 4:10)
      3) Demas (Philemon 24, Colossians 4:14)
      4) Luke (Philemon 24, Colossians 4:14)
      5) Jesus, called Justus (Colossians 4:11)
      6) Epaphroditus (Philippians 2:25-30; 4:18)

4. Paul preached boldly in Rome.
   a. Colossians 1:17-29; 4:3-4
   b. Ephesians 3:7-9; 6:18-20
   c. Philippians 1:12-18

5. Paul maintained a right spirit in his suffering.
   a. Colossians 1:24
   b. Ephesians 3:13
   c. Philippians 2:16-18; 3:7-21; 4:11-13

6. Paul loved and cared for the Church
   a. Colossians 1:1-9; 2:1-5; 4:15-17
   b. Ephesians 1:15-16; 3:14-21
   c. Philippians 1:1-11, 27; 2:12; 2:16-18; 4:10, 14, 17

Lesson 7
Study Questions

1.   Who accompanied Paul from Caesarea to Rome?

2.   How do we know Luke went with Paul?

3.   From where was Aristarchus?

4.   What was the centurion's name?

5.   How did he show kindness to Paul?

6.   Where did the Alexandrian ship stop?

7.   What did Paul want to do?

8.   What did he say about the trip?

9.   Why did the centurion not listen to Paul?

10.   What took the ship off course?

11.   What did Paul say to encourage the men?

12.   How did he know?

13. What three things did the angel say?

14. How long did the storm last?

15. For what did the men pray?

16. Why did the soldiers let the lifeboat fall away?

17. What did Paul urge the men to do?

18. How many men were there aboard ship?

19. What did the men decide to do?

20. What happened when the ship ran aground?

21. Why were the soldiers ready to kill the prisoners?

22. Why did the centurion stop them?

23. How many people got to shore safely?

24. What was the name of the island?

25. What sort of people lived there?

26. What happened to Paul there?

27. What did the people first think?

28. Why did they change their minds?

29. What did they think next?

30. Who was Publius?

31. What did Paul do for him?

32. How did Paul and his company win favor with the people?

33. Where did Paul go next?

34. Where did Paul find brothers?

35. Who greeted Paul at Rome?

36. How did Paul respond?

37. Where did Paul stay in Rome?

38. Who are the first members of the church in Rome greeted by Paul?

39. Who was Epenetus?

40. Who did Paul say were outstanding among the apostles?

41. What could have been significant about Rufus?

42. Whom did Paul call together in Rome?

43. Why did he call them?

44. Did they have a bad report about Paul?

45. Of what did they have a bad report?

46. What did the leaders want to do?

47. Of what did Paul explain and declare to them?

48. Of what did he try to convince them?

49. How did they respond?

50. Who did Paul quote?

51. What would happen if the leaders would see, hear, and understand?

52. What did Paul say about God's salvation?

53. What two things did Paul preach and teach about?

54. For how long?

55. In what manner?

56. What are the four "Prison Epistles"?

57.   Of what two things do they confirm?

58.   Name the members of Paul's Roman company.

59.   Who was Epaphras?

60.   Who was the runaway slave?

61.   Who was the bearer of the letter to the Colossians?

62.   What is significant about Mark's presence with Paul?

63.   What does Paul call Luke in Colossians 4:14?

64.   What three important facts concerning Paul are revealed in the "Prison Epistles"?

65.   What three things should we be doing today?

Lesson Eight
VIII. PAUL'S CLOSING YEARS OF MINISTRY (I & II Timothy, Titus, Portions of the "Prison Epistles")

A. Theories Concerning Paul's Final Years
 1. Paul's ministry and life closes with the book of Acts.
  a. He was imprisoned for two years in Rome. (Acts 28:30)
  b. He died in prison awaiting trial, or
  c. He was martyred by the emperor Nero about 64 A.D. after the great fire and persecution of Roman Christians.
  d. Problems with the theory:
   1) If this theory is accurate, then Paul could not have been the author of the "Pastoral Epistles" (I & II Timothy and Titus) **or:**
   2) Events recorded in the "Pastoral Epistles" had to have occurred much earlier in Paul's ministry and cannot be supported by the Book of Acts or any other epistle.

 2. There were two separate imprisonments of Paul.
  a. Paul spent two years in Roman captivity, where he wrote the "Prison Epistles" (Philemon, Colossians, Philippians, and Ephesians).
  b. He was released about 63 A.D.
  c. He spent the next few years traveling in ministry and wrote I Timothy and Titus.
  d. Paul was again arrested and taken to Rome where he wrote II Timothy while awaiting his ultimate execution.
  e. The only problem with this theory is that nothing is recorded in Acts about Paul's life after his first imprisonment. However, Luke does not record everything that Paul did when compared to Paul's own epistles.
  f. Ultimately, the Pastoral Epistles can only make sense if there were, indeed, two separate imprisonments.

B. Paul's Ministry after His Release, 63-67 A.D.

 1. Paul continued to preach the gospel.
  a. I Timothy 2:7; 4:10
  b. Titus 1:1-3

 2. Paul had companions during this period:
  a. Timothy (I Timothy 1:1-2)
   1) He was Paul's true son in the faith.
   2) He was left by Paul in Ephesus to instruct the church there.

  b. Titus (Titus 1:4-5)
   1) He was Paul's true son in their common faith.
   2) He was left by Paul in Crete to straighten out what was left unfinished and to appoint elders in every town.
   3) He later went to Dalmatia. (II Timothy 4:10)

c. Artemas   (Titus 3:12) was to be sent by Paul (as a replacement for Titus).
d. Tychicus (Titus 3:12)
  1) He was an alternate to Artemas.
  2) He was later sent by Paul to Ephesus. (II Timothy 4:12)

e. Zenas (Titus 3:13), was a lawyer to be helped by Titus.
f. Apollos (Titus 3:13) was also to be helped by Titus (we met Apollos in Acts 18:24).
g. Onesiphorus (II Timothy 1:16-18)
  1) He often refreshed Paul.
  2) He was not ashamed of Paul's chains.
  3) He searched hard to find Paul in Rome.
  4) He helped Paul in Ephesus.

h. Demas (II Timothy 4:10)
  1) He loved this world.
  2) He deserted Paul to Thessalonica.

i. Crescens (II Timothy 4:10) went to Galatia.
j. Luke (II Timothy 4:11)
k. Mark (II Timothy 4:11) was asked for by Paul.
l. Carpus (II Timothy 4:13) had Paul's cloak in Troas.
m. Priscilla and Aquila (II Timothy 4:19) were greeted by Paul.
n. Erastus (II Timothy 4:20) stayed in Corinth.
o. Trophimus (II Timothy 4:20) was left by Paul, sick in Miletus.
p. Others with Paul:
  1) Eubulus
  2) Pudens
  3) Linus
  4) Claudia

3. Paul had enemies during this period.
  a. Alexander, the coppersmith (I Timothy 1:19-20, II Timothy 4:14)
    1) He reflected faith and a good conscience.
    2) He shipwrecked his faith.
    3) He was "handed over to Satan" to be taught not to blaspheme.
    4) He did Paul much evil.

  b. Hymenaeus (I Timothy 1:19-20, II Timothy 2:16-18)
    1) He was included with Alexander.
    2) His teaching (Godless chatter) was spreading like gangrene.
    3) He wandered from the truth.
    4) He said the resurrection had already occurred.
    5) He destroyed the faith of some.

  c. Philetus (II Timothy 2:17-18) was a cohort of Hymenaeus.

4. Paul traveled extensively during this period.
   a. While writing during his first imprisonment, he intended to visit several places, including:
      1) Philippi (Philippians 1:26, 2:24)
      2) Colossae (Philemon 22)
      3) Laodicea (Colossians 2:1, 4:13)
      4) Hierapolis (Colossians 4:13)
      5) Spain (Romans 15:24, 28)

   b. Paul, in fact, did visit many places after he was freed. While we can't be sure concerning the above intended visits, we can substantiate those below:
      1) Ephesus (I Timothy 1:3); he left Timothy here.
      2) Macedonia (I Timothy 1:3, 3:14); he wrote to Timothy from here.
      3) Crete (Titus 1:5); Paul left Titus in charge of the churches here.
      4) Miletus (II Timothy 4:20); Paul left Trophimus sick here.
      5) Troas (II Timothy 4:13); Paul left his cloak and some parchments with Carpus here.
      6) Corinth (II Timothy 4:20); he was with Erastus.
      7) Nicopolis (Titus 3:12); Paul intended to winter here.

C. Paul's Final Imprisonment (II Timothy)

   1. Paul was imprisoned. (II Timothy 1:8)
      a. He was chained as a criminal. (II Timothy 2:9)
      b. He was difficult to locate. (II Timothy 1:17)
      c. No one dared support him. (II Timothy 4:16)
      d. He didn't expect to survive. (II Timothy 4:6-8)

   2. Paul was lonely.
      a. His friends were on missions.
         1) Tychicus was in Ephesus. (II Timothy 4:12)
         2) Erastus was in Corinth. (II Timothy 4:20)
         3) Trophimus was in Miletus. (II Timothy 4:20)
         4) Priscilla and Aquila were gone. (II Timothy 4:19)
         5) Titus was in Dalmatia. (II Timothy 4:10)
         6) Crescens was in Galatia. (II Timothy 4:10)
         7) Luke, alone, was still with him. (II Timothy 4:11)

      b. Some former co-workers had deserted him:
         1) Demas (II Timothy 4:10)
         2) Phygelus (II Timothy 1:15)
         3) Herogenes (II Timothy 1:15)
         4) Everyone in the Province of Asia (II Timothy 1:15)

c. He sorely missed Timothy and Mark. (II Timothy 1:3-4; 4:9, 11, 21)
d. He asked for a few of his personal effects: (II Timothy 4:13)
   1) A cloak
   2) Scrolls
   3) Parchments

3. Paul's last thoughts
   a. He wanted to encourage Timothy:
      1) To re-fire his gift (II Timothy 1:6)
      2) To join Paul's suffering in testimony of the gospel (II Timothy 1:8)
      3) To keep sound teaching with faith and love in Christ (II Timothy 1:13)
      4) To be strong in the grace of Christ Jesus (II Timothy 2:1)
      5) To entrust to reliable men Paul's words (II Timothy 2:2)
      6) To endure hardship: (II Timothy 2:3-6)
         a) As a soldier
         b) As an athlete
         c) As a farmer

      7) To present himself as a workman who correctly handles the Word of God
         (II Timothy 2:15)
      8) To flee from the evil desires of the youth (II Timothy 2:22)
      9) To not be quarrelsome (II Timothy 2:23-26)
      10) To continue in what he has learned (II Timothy 3:14)
      11) To preach the Word, correct, rebuke, and encourage with great patience and careful
         instruction (II Timothy 4:2)
      12) To do the work of an evangelist, discharging all the duties of his ministry (II Timothy 4:5)

   b. He was ready to die for Christ's sake.
      1) He was not ashamed, convinced Christ would guard what Paul had entrusted to Him.
         (II Timothy 1:12)
      2) He was able to endure everything for the sake of the elect. (II Timothy 2:10)
      3) He was already poured out like a drink offering, and the time had come for his departure.
         (II Timothy 4:6)
      4) He had completed his mission: (II Timothy 4:7-8)
         a) He had fought the good fight.
         b) He had finished the race.
         c) He had kept the faith.
         d) He was ready to receive the crown of righteousness as his reward.

      5) He believed that he would be rescued by the Lord from every evil attack to bring him
         safely to his heavenly Kingdom. (II Timothy 4:18)

Lesson Eight
Study Questions

1. Why do many scholars believe that Paul was imprisoned more than once in Rome?

2. Name the Pastoral Epistles.

3. Name the Prison Epistles.

4. When did Paul probably write I Timothy and Titus?

5. When did Paul probably write II Timothy?

6. What did Paul do while free?

7. Which two men did Paul refer to as his sons in the faith?

8. Where did Paul leave Timothy?

9. Where did Paul leave Titus?

10. Where did Titus finally end up?

11. Who were replacements for Titus?

12. Who was not ashamed of Paul's chains?

13. Who loved the world and deserted Paul?

14.   Whom did Paul tell Timothy to bring to him?

15.   What married couple did Paul greet?

16.   Who were Paul's three chief enemies?

17.   What was Hymenaeus' false teaching about the resurrection?

18.   Name three places Paul had intended to visit when he was released.

19.   From where did Paul write I Timothy?

20.   Where did he leave "sick" Trophimus?

21.   Where did Paul leave his cloak?

22.   Where did Paul intend to spend the winter?

23.   How was Paul treated during his second imprisonment?

24.   Do you think he expected to be freed again?

25.   Why was Paul lonely?

26.   What three things did he ask Timothy to bring to him?

27.   In what did Paul ask Timothy to join him?

28. What was Timothy to do with Paul's words?

29. What three occupations does Paul use to illustrate enduring hardships?

30. From what was Timothy to flee?

31. What do you suppose they are?

32. What four things was Timothy to do in his authority?

33. In what manner was he to do these things?

34. What did Paul imply Timothy's ministry was?

35. In what four ways had Paul completed his mission?

36. For whose sake was Paul willing to endure everything?

37. With what sort of offering did he compare his life?

38. What time did he say had come?

39. He believed the Lord would rescue him from what?

40. To where did Paul expect the Lord to bring him?

The Life and Ministry of Paul
Answer Key

Lesson One

1. Tarsus of Cilicia
2. Benjamin
3. Gamaliel
4. Pharisees
5. (1) He was a zealous Jew (2) didn't yet have faith (3) didn't know what he was doing
6. He watched the witness' clothes and he approved of Stephen's murder
7. He had them imprisoned, beat them, testified against them, pursued them, persecuted them
8. Damascus
9. To show Paul that Jesus is a light brighter than the sun (answers may vary)
10. To show that unbelievers are blind to the true light (answers may vary)
11. He was healed, commissioned, baptized, and filled with the Holy Spirit
12. (Answers will vary)
13. It made him an apostle
14. People wanted to kill him
15. Peter
16. Barnabas
17. God warned him in a trance
18. Syria and Cilicia
19. Barnabas
20. Antioch - taught the church a whole year
21. To bring money to the church there
22. John Mark

Lesson Two

1. The teachers and prophets at the church in Antioch
2. The Holy Spirit told them
3. They fasted and prayed, then laid hands on them
4. To Cyprus
5. Preached the Word of God in the synagogues
6. A Jewish magician who pretended to be a prophet
7. He was made blind by Paul's curse
8. He was trying to frustrate the work of God
9. The governor of Cyprus
10. He saw what happened to Bar-Jesus and was amazed at the teachings about Jesus
11. John Mark left Paul and Barnabas and went home to Jerusalem
12. The officials of the synagogue
13. They invited Paul and Barnabas back again
14. Almost the whole town

15. To hear the Word of the Lord
16. They became jealous and disputed and insulted Paul
17. They said they would go to the Gentiles
18. Those who had been chosen for eternal life
19. The Word of God spread everywhere
20. They shook the dust off their feet in protest
21. To Iconium
22. The same thing that happened at Antioch
23. He gave them the power to perform miracles and wonders
24. They had learned of the plan to mistreat and stone them
25. To the cities of Lystra and Derbe in Lycaonia
26. Paul healed a lame man
27. To announce the good news, and to turn the people away from worthless things to the living God
28. The Jews from Antioch of Pisidia and Iconium
29. Preached the good news and won many disciples
30. Lystra, Iconium, and Antioch of Pisidia
31. Many troubles
32. 2 Timothy 3:10-11
33. The Lord rescued him
34. Antioch of Syria

Lesson Three

1. That you had to be circumcised to be saved
2. No, they argued fiercely against them
3. Paul, Barnabas, and others be sent to see the apostles and elders in Jerusalem about it
4. Titus
5. God revealed to him that he should go
6. They had great joy
7. They were pretending to be fellow believers; they were spies on Paul's freedom in Christ; they wanted to enslave believers
8. To keep the truth of the gospel safe
9. He gave them the Holy Spirit
10. Because they believed
11. Amos
12. That the apostles shouldn't "trouble" the Gentiles who were turning to God
13. (Answers will vary)
14. Food offered to idols, sexual immorality, eating animals which have been strangled, and eating blood
15. Judas Barsabbas and Silas
16. The apostles and elders
17. They had authority that was recognized by all the churches (they were apostles)
18. James'
19. Only, "keep from sexual immorality"
20. Galatians 2:6-10
21. Peter

22. That Paul and Barnabas would work among the Gentiles, and James, Peter and John would work among the Jews
23. Not at all
24. Both were apostles by God's power
25. Gathered the believers and read them the apostle's letter
26. With great joy
27. They were prophets
28. Taught and preached the Word of God
29. He was afraid to eat with the Gentiles after the Jews arrived (hypocrisy)
30. Not walking in a straight path in line with the truth of the gospel

Lesson Four

1. To visit brothers from every city where they had preached
2. They argued over whether to take Mark
3. He had deserted them earlier
4. Silas
5. Through Syria and Cilicia
6. Strengthened churches
7. Lystra
8. All the believers in Lystra and Iconium spoke well of him
9. Because the Jews there knew Timothy's father was a Greek
10. The rules the elders and apostles had decided were necessary
11. The Holy Spirit wouldn't allow them
12. The Spirit of Jesus wouldn't let them go to Bithynia
13. To Troas
14. A Macedonian begging for help
15. To go preach the good news in Macedonia
16. Philippi
17. That's where the Jews gathered for prayer
18. She was a dealer of purple cloth
19. The Lord opened her mind to what Paul was saying
20. The same way as with Lydia
21. She and the people of her house were baptized
22. Silas, Timothy, Luke, Clement, Euodia and Syntyche
23. Luke wrote Acts and says "we" left for Troas and on to Macedonia
24. She was able to tell fortunes for money
25. That they were servants of the most high God, and were announcing how one could be saved
26. Yes, but they are not saved because they don't obey God (answers may vary)
27. Cast out the evil spirit
28. They realized their profit was gone
29. That they caused trouble by teaching Jewish customs against Roman Law
30. No, they were angry over losing profit
31. The owners
32. No
33. Too easily

34. It is not good
35. They were beaten and jailed by the officials
36. Prayed and sang praises to God
37. Rejoice that you participate in the sufferings of Christ
38. A violent earthquake
39. He thought the prisoners had escaped
40. "What must I do to be saved?"
41. "Believe in the Lord Jesus, and you and your family will be saved."
42. They were all baptized
43. Because they now believed in God
44. They learned that they had punished Roman citizens
45. They went to apologize, led them out of prison, and asked them to leave the city
46. They encouraged the believers at Lydia's house
47. At the synagogue
48. The jealous Jews
49. By saying there was another King -- Jesus
50. He was not lazy, paid his own way, worked night and day so as not to be
    an expense to anyone, etc.
51. "Whoever refuses to work is not allowed to eat"
52. Yes. They shouldn't be a burden on others (answers will vary)
53. (Answers will vary)
54. Because God judges our motives (He knows our heart)
55. He didn't use flattering talk, had no disguised greed, and made no attempt to get praise
56. No (answers will vary)
57. His love for them
58. (Answers will vary)
59. His own and the Lord's
60. They put it into practice
61. By putting our faith into practice
62. Because the Jews were looking for them
63. Open-minded people
64. They studied the scriptures every day
65. Jews from Thessalonica
66. Athens
67. That there were so many idols
68. In the synagogue and in the marketplace
69. Because he was teaching about Christ and the resurrection
70. The Aeropagus
71. The maker of the world and everything in it, the Lord of Heaven and earth
72. Nothing
73. We are His children
74. Turn away from their evil (repent)
75. By raising him from the dead
76. Some made fun of him; some wanted to hear more; some joined him and believed
77. The same as above (answers will vary)
78. Aquila and Priscilla

79. He was a tentmaker
80. To remove any obstacle in the way of the gospel
81. From Corinth
82. He shook the dust off his clothes and told them he could take no blame for their fate
83. Go to the Gentiles
84. Next to the synagogue
85. Crispus, Gaius, and Stephanas
86. Don't be afraid; keep speaking; don't give up; I am with you; No one will be able to harm you; there are many of my people in this city
87. Paul was going to be taken before the Roman Governor (answers may vary)
88. (Answers will vary)
89. One and a half years
90. He threw the case out of court
91. Nothing
92. Aquila and Priscilla
93. He had fulfilled a vow
94. In Ephesus
95. That he would return if it was God's will
96. He greeted the church there
97. Antioch
98. Strengthened all the believers

Lesson Five

1. An eloquent speaker, had a thorough knowledge of the scriptures; he had been instructed in the way of the Lord
2. He knew only the baptism of John (hadn't received the baptism of the Holy Spirit)
3. Aquila and Priscilla
4. Go to Achaia (Corinth)
5. They wrote letters asking the Corinthians to welcome him
6. He helped new believers and he defeated the Jews in public debate using the scripture to prove Jesus is the Messiah
7. They had not received the Holy Spirit
8. A baptism of repentance
9. The Holy Spirit came upon them, they spoke in tongues, and prophesied
10. Three months
11. About the Kingdom of God
12. Because some would not believe and spoke evil of the way of the Lord
13. At the lecture hall of Tyrannus
14. For two years
15. Miracles were happening
16. No
17. Attacked them with violence
18. Yes (answers will vary)
19. Believers confessed their sins (evil deeds) in public and magicians burned their books in public
20. (Answers will vary)

21. To take an offering to the church there
22. Timothy and Erastus
23. To Corinth
24. Because of Timothy's faithful service to him
25. Titus
26. Because he and the other idol makers might lose business, and the goddess Artemis would lose her temple if people were converted to God
27. Gaius and Aristarchus
28. Some of the believers and friends who were authorities
29. Because most of the crowd didn't know what was going on
30. No (answers will vary)
31. He was a Jew (they knew he didn't want idols)
32. The city clerk
33. That everything should be settled in a legal meeting
34. No (answers will vary)
35. Repent and believe in our Lord Jesus
36. To watch over their flock (be shepherds) and themselves
37. The care of God and the message of grace
38. He wanted to be an example (answers will vary)
39. (Answers will vary)
40. To preach the gospel
41. Timothy and Titus
42. Corinth
43. It's generosity
44. (Answers will vary)
45. To continue the work there, to collect an offering for the church in Judea, and to deliver Paul's letter
46. The epistle to the Romans
47. Phoebe
48. He was city treasurer
49. (Answers will vary)
50. To deliver an offering from the churches at Macedonia and Achaia
51. He begins to use "we" again (remember, Luke wrote the Book of Acts)
52. He was raised from the dead by Paul when he fell from the third story window
53. To save time; he wanted to reach Jerusalem before Pentecost
54. At Miletus
55. Repent from sin and believe in the Lord Jesus
56. (Answers will vary)
57. To finish the work the Lord Jesus gave him to do
58. The same
59. The Kingdom of God
60. Shepherds of the Church of God
61. It is able to build you up and give you God's blessing
62. He worked for them
63. (Answers will vary)
64. Paul said they wouldn't see him again

65. That Paul was not to go to Jerusalem
66. (Answers will vary)
67. They had the gift of prophecy?
68. Yes
69. That he would be bound by the Jews and delivered to the Gentiles
70. That he was ready to die for the sake of the Lord Jesus

Lesson Six

1. Warmly
2. James
3. Praised God
4. They had been told that Paul was teaching Jews to turn from the Law of Moses (not to circumcise or live by Jewish customs)
5. (Answers will vary)
6. (Answers will vary)
7. To disprove the bad report about Paul
8. Abstain from (1) food sacrificed to idols (2) meat from strangled animals (3) blood (4) sexual immorality
9. (Answers will vary)
10. Yes, he followed the instructions; no, he was seized by the Jews
11. Some Jews from the province of Asia
12. Teaching against the Jews, the Law, and the temple; and defiling the temple by bringing a Greek into it.
13. Seized him, dragged him from the temple and tried to kill him
14. The Roman commander came with soldiers
15. Arrested him, bound him with chains, and questioned the crowd about him
16. The confusion and violence of the crowd was great
17. About his Jewish background, how he had persecuted the saints, and his Damascus Road experience
18. Paul, alone
19. Ananias
20. A devout observer of the Law, highly respected by all the Jews
21. (1) he was chosen by God (2) he was to know God's will, see the Righteous One, and hear His words (3) he would be His witness to all men (4) he should be baptized and call on the name of Jesus
22. Leave Jerusalem immediately, that his testimony would be rejected
23. To the Gentiles
24. For him to be killed
25. He found that Paul was a Roman citizen and he had bound him and almost flogged him illegally
26. To determine the nature of the Jewish accusations against Paul
27. That he had fulfilled his duty to God in good conscience
28. Had Paul struck in the mouth
29. He was judging Paul by the Law while breaking it himself
30. He didn't know Ananias was the high priest and didn't want to speak evil of a ruler of the people
31. To create a controversy in the Sanhedrin
32. The Pharisees believed in resurrection, but the Sadducees did not

33. The dispute between the Pharisees and Sadducees became so violent he feared Paul would be harmed
34. (Answers will vary)
35. Testify about him in Rome as he had in Jerusalem
36. Not to eat or drink until Paul was killed
37. Trick the Roman commander to bring Paul out so they could ambush him
38. Of course not!
39. Their own
40. Always try to please God by obeying Him (answers may vary)
41. Paul's nephew told him and the commander
42. To Caesarea
43. To protect him from the Jews
44. Because he was a Roman citizen
45. Not worthwhile to punish Paul
46. Ananias the high priest, some elders, and Tertullus the lawyer
47. (1) Being a troublemaker (2) stirring up riots among the Jews (3) being a ringleader of the Nazarene sect (4) trying to desecrate the temple
48. To worship
49. The "Way"
50. The God of our fathers
51. The Law and the prophets
52. To bring gifts to the poor and offerings
53. The Jews from Asia who seized him
54. His belief in the resurrection of the dead
55. Yes, he was well acquainted with it
56. Felix's wife, a Jewess
57. Faith in Jesus Christ
58. Paul talked about righteousness, self-control, and the judgment
59. Answers will vary
60. He wanted a bribe
61. He wanted to do a favor for the Jews
62. Porcius Festus
63. So they might ambush and kill him
64. To bring charges against Paul
65. No
66. No
67. He was a Roman citizen
68. He appealed to Caesar
69. To send him to Caesar
70. King Agrippa and his wife Bernice
71. Religious disputes
72. To hear Paul, himself
73. Help in determining what charges to specify against Paul to Caesar
74. He was well acquainted with Jewish customs and controversies
75. A servant and a witness

76. (1) To open their eyes (2) to turn them from darkness to light (3) to turn them from the power of God to Satan (4) to make possible forgiveness of sins and a place among those sanctified by faith in Christ
77. Repentance and turning to God with good deeds
78. (1) He would suffer (2) He would be the first to rise from the dead
    (3) He would proclaim light to His own people (4) He would proclaim light to the Gentiles
79. His great learning had driven him insane
80. If he believed the prophets
81. If Paul was trying to make him a Christian
82. He wished everyone would become Christians
83. Paul was innocent of anything that deserved death
84. He had appealed to Caesar
85. Answers will vary

Lesson Seven

1. Aristarchus and Luke
2. The "we" in Acts 27:1 (Luke wrote Acts)
3. Thessalonica
4. Julius
5. Allowed Paul to see his friends and to have his needs met
6. At Fair Havens in Crete
7. Winter at Fair Havens
8. It would be disastrous
9. The pilot an ship owner said that Fair Havens was not suitable for wintering
10. Hurricane force winds (a northeaster)
11. None would be lost
12. An angel had appeared to him
13. (1) Do not be afraid (2) you must stand trial before Caesar (3) God has graciously given you the lives of all who sail with you
14. Fourteen days
15. Daylight
16. So he sailors couldn't desert the others
17. To eat
18. 276
19. Run the ship aground at a sandy beach on an island
20. It broke into pieces
21. To prevent them from escaping
22. He wanted to save Paul's live
23. All of them
24. Malta
25. Unusually kind people
26. He was bitten by a viper
27. Justice was catching up to him because he was a murderer
28. He suffered no ill effects
29. He was a god

30. The chief official of the island
31. Healed his father
32. They cured the rest of the sick on the island
33. Syracuse for three days
34. Puteoli
35. More brothers
36. He thanked God and was encouraged
37. By himself with a guard
38. Priscilla and Aquila
39. The first convert from Asia
40. Andronicus and Junias
41. He was son of Simon of Cyrene who carried the cross of Jesus
42. The leaders of the Jews
43. To explain his situation
44. No
45. Paul's sect
46. To hear Paul's view
47. The Kingdom of God
48. Jesus
49. Some were convinced, some did not believe
50. Isaiah
51. They would turn and be healed by God
52. It had been sent to the Gentiles
53. The Kingdom and Lord Jesus Christ
54. Two years
55. Boldly and without hindrance
56. Philemon, Colossians, Ephesians and Philippians
57. Paul was a prisoner and expected to be released
58. Timothy, Epaphras, Onesimus, Tychicus, Mark, Aristarchus, Demas, Luke, Jesus (called Justus), and Epaphroditus
59. The evangelist who founded the church at Colossae
60. Onesimus
61. Tychicus
62. Paul and Barnabas had separated over taking Mark along on the second missionary journey; they must have been reconciled
63. The doctor
64. (1) He preached boldly (2) he maintained a right spirit in his suffering (3) he loved and cared for the church
65. The same

Lesson Eight

1. Because the "pastoral epistles" contain events that could not have happened before Paul's first imprisonment recorded in Acts
2. 1Timothy, 2 Timothy, and Titus
3. Philemon, Colossians, Philippians, and Ephesians

4. Between the time of his first imprisonment and his second imprisonment in Rome
5. During his second imprisonment
6. Continued to preach the gospel
7. Timothy and Titus
8. In Ephesus
9. In Crete
10. In Dalmatia
11. Tychicus or Artemas
12. Onesiphorus
13. Demas
14. Mark
15. Priscilla and Aquila
16. Alexander, Hymenaeus, and Philetus
17. It had already happened
18. Philippi, Colossae, Laodicea, Hierapolis, Spain
19. Macedonia
20. Miletus
21. Troas
22. Nicopolis
23. Like a criminal
24. No
25. His friends were away and some had deserted him
26. His cloak, scrolls, and parchments
27. In his suffering
28. To entrust him to reliable men
29. Soldier, athlete, farmer
30. The evil desires of the youth
31. (Answers will vary)
32. (1) Preach the Word (2) correct (3) rebuke (4) encourage
33. With great patience and careful instruction
34. An evangelist
35. (1) fought the good fight (2) finished the race (3) kept the faith
    (4) ready to receive the crown of righteousness as his reward
36. For the elect
37. A drink offering (poured out)
38. The time for his departure
39. Every evil attack
40. Safely to His heavenly Kingdom

The Life and Ministry of Paul
Exam #1
Lessons One through Four

Multiple Choice:

1. Paul was born in
   a. Tarsus of Cilicia
   b. Antioch of Pisidia
   c. Antioch of Syria
   d. Bethlehem of Judea
   e. Jerusalem of Judea

2. Paul was a Jew from the tribe of
   a. Ephraim
   b. Dan
   c. Judah
   d. Levi
   e. none of the above

3. Paul was feared by the Christians because
   a. he imprisoned them
   b. he beat them
   c. he testified against them
   d. he pursued them abroad
   e. all of the above

4. Paul's teacher was named
   a. Ananias
   b. Gamaliel
   c. Luke
   d. Apollos
   e. none of the above

5. Paul's conversion experience happened on the road to
   a. Jerusalem
   b. Jericho
   c. Damascus
   d. Antioch
   e. Bethlehem

6. From his youth Paul had been trained as a
   a. Christian
   b. Sadducee
   c. Gnostic
   d. Pharisee
   e. none of the above

7. Previous to his conversion Paul had been
   a. righteous and zealous
   b. a liar and a thief
   c. an enemy of Judaism
   d. a Roman soldier
   e. none of the above

8. In Paul's vision who spoke to him?
   a. Jesus, Himself
   b. Ananias
   c. an angel of the Lord
   d. Stephen's ghost
   e. all of the above

9. Paul later claimed to be a true apostle because
   a. he had conferred with the original disciples
   b. he had seen Jesus face to face
   c. he spoke God's word boldly
   d. he knew he would die for Christ
   e. all of the above

10. Who was sent to Antioch to seek Paul?
    a. James
    b. Silas
    c. Barnabas
    d. Timothy
    e. John Mark

11. Paul and Barnabas were chosen and sent
    a. from the church at Antioch
    b. by prophets and teachers
    c. by laying on of hands
    d. through the leading of the Holy Spirit
    e. all of the above

12. Paul's first stop on his first missionary journey was
    a. Salamis on the Island of Crete
    b. Paphos on the Island of Cyprus
    c. Seleucia on the Island of Cyprus
    d. Salamis on the Island of Cyprus
    e. none of the above

13. Bar-Jesus, known as Elymas
    a. lived in Paphos
    b. was a Jew
    c. pretended to be a prophet
    d. was a friend of the governor
    e. all of the above

14. Sergius Paulus
    a. was Governor of Seleucia
    b. believed when he saw Elymas blinded
    c. rejected the Word of God
    d. called the magician "son of the devil"
    e. all of the above

15. Because of the large crowds coming to hear Paul at the synagogue at Antioch of Pisidia
    a. the Jews became jealous
    b. the whole city was saved
    c. the governor closed down the meeting
    d. Paul was asked to become Pastor there
    e. none of the above

16. Paul and Barnabas were thrown out of Antioch of Pisidia when
    a. they refused to get a license to meet
    b. they wouldn't attend the mayor's address
    c. the Jews stirred up important people against them
    d. they were discovered to be Jews
    e. none of the above

17. When Paul and Barnabas went to a new city, they always began preaching
    a. at the synagogue
    b. at the market
    c. at the local government center
    d. at the football stadium
    e. at the prison

18. When Paul and Barnabas preached boldly, God proved their message by
    a. causing the people to repent
    b. soothing the anger of the Jews
    c. blessing them with finances
    d. giving them power to do miracles
    e. all of the above

19. When Paul and Barnabas went to Lystra
    a. they preached the Good News
    b. they healed a lame man
    c. they were mistaken for gods
    d. none of the above
    e. all of the above

20. At Derbe, Paul taught that in order to enter the Kingdom of God we must
    a. be born again
    b. be filled with the Holy Spirit
    c. pass through many troubles
    d. pray without ceasing
    e. all of the above

21. Paul remembered later that during his first journey
    a. he had no problems
    b. the Lord rescued him from all his problems
    c. God protected him from being persecuted
    d. those to whom he preached were always a blessing
    e. all of the above

22. The main issue brought up by the Jewish Christians was
    a. the authority of a believer
    b. tithes and offerings
    c. baptism by immersion
    d. circumcision for new believers
    e. none of the above

23. According to Paul, those insisting on circumcision
    a. were pretending to be fellow believers
    b. were spies on his freedom
    c. wanted to enslave believers to the Law of Moses
    d. none of the above
    e. all of the above

24. At the Council at Jerusalem
    a. Peter suggested that a letter of instruction be sent to the Gentiles
    b. James said he was chosen once to preach to Gentiles
    c. it was decided not to trouble Gentile believers with circumcision
    d. Paul and Silas reported their work to the apostles
    e. all of the above

25. Of the necessary rules given to Gentile believers by the Council, the only one that Paul supported in later writings was
    a. not to eat food offered to idols
    b. to avoid sexual immorality
    c. not to eat blood
    d. not to eat animals which have been strangled
    e. all of the above

26. Paul recognized later that God's power had made him
    a. an apostle to the Gentiles
    b. a living epistle to the Jews
    c. a thorn in the side of Jews
    d. the foremost minister of the gospel
    e. all of the above

27. Later Paul had a quarrel with Peter because
    a. Peter was afraid of appearances
    b. Peter wanted to force Gentiles to live like Jews
    c. Peter wouldn't eat with Gentiles if Jews were present
    d. Peter was not walking in a straight path
    e. all of the above

28. Peter did agree that God had showed His approval to the Gentile believers by
    a. sending Paul to them
    b. giving them the Holy Spirit
    c. drawing them together to hear His word
    d. sending prophets and teachers among them
    e. all of the above

29. Barnabas and Paul separated because
    a. Paul wanted to take Timothy to visit churches
    b. Paul wanted to take John Mark to visit churches
    c. Barnabas wanted to take Silas to visit churches
    d. Barnabas wanted to take Timothy to visit churches
    e. none of the above

30. Timothy
    a. had a Greek mother and Jewish father
    b. was from Tarsus
    c. was circumcised by Paul
    d. became a Christian under Paul's ministry
    e. all of the above

31. While at Troas, Paul had a vision of
    a. an angel warning him not to go into Asia
    b. of a Macedonian begging for them to come and help
    c. of the Lord telling Paul he would suffer
    d. of his mother asking why he hadn't visited her
    e. none of the above

32. Lydia
    a. was a tentmaker like Paul
    b. was afraid to be baptized
    c. was from Corinth
    d. asked Paul's team to stay with her in Philippi
    e. all of the above

33. Paul's team in Philippi included
    a. Luke
    b. Barnabas
    c. Apollos
    d. John Mark
    e. all of the above

34. Paul and Silas were beaten and jailed in Philippi because
    a. they were teaching customs against Roman Law
    b. they were Jews
    c. they were preaching without official permission
    d. they cast an evil spirit out of a fortune-telling slave girl
    e. all of the above

35. While Paul and Silas were in jail
    a. They prayed and sang praises
    b. an earthquake shook the jail
    c. chains fell off all the prisoners
    d. the doors opened
    e. all of the above

36. The question the jailor at Philippi asked was
    a. Who is going to pay for all this damage?
    b. What must I do to be saved?
    c. What am I going to tell the Chief?
    d. Who are you people, anyway?
    e. none of the above

37. Paul and Silas refused to leave the jail because
    a. they weren't guilty of anything
    b. they wanted to be released by the officials publicly
    c. they had been falsely imprisoned
    d. they had been whipped in public although being Roman citizens
    e. all of the above

38. At Thessalonica
    a. a large number of Greeks joined Paul's group
    b. there was no interest in the gospel
    c. an angry mob stoned Paul
    d. Paul was well-supported by the people
    e. all of the above

39. Concerning work Paul taught
    a. that pastors need not work
    b. that work is a curse of God
    c. that work is foolish since Christ will return soon
    d. that whoever refuses to work should not be allowed to eat
    e. none of the above

40. Paul compared his relationship with the Thessalonians to that of
    a. a commander and his army
    b. a farmer and his harvest
    c. a mother and her children
    d. a shepherd and his sheep
    e. none of the above

41. Later, in order to strengthen the church at Thessalonica, Paul sent them
    a. roofing sheets
    b. a love offering of money
    c. Timothy
    d. a strong word of prophecy
    e. none of the above

42. The Bereans were special to Paul because
    a. they gave Paul a nice offering
    b. they studied the scriptures daily
    c. they always agreed with him
    d. they built him a nice church building
    e. all of the above

43. In Athens, Paul held discussions with
    a. the Jews
    b. the Gentiles who worshiped God
    c. with passers-by in the market place
    d. with certain philosophers
    e. all of the above

44. At Athens, Paul was invited to speak before the
    a. synagogue
    b. Senate
    c. mayor
    d. Aeropagus
    e. none of the above

45. Paul told the people at Athens that the "unknown" God was
    a. the maker of the world and everything in it
    b. the Lord of heaven and earth
    c. not living in man-made temples
    d. gives us life, breath, and everything else
    e. all of the above

46. Paul preached to the people in Athens that God has commanded men to turn away from their evil deeds because
    a. He has fixed a day of judgment
    b. His mercy is everlasting
    c. He wants people to be nice
    d. He is tired of their idolatry
    e. none of the above

47. Aquila and Priscilla
    a. were living in Athens
    b. were dealers in purple dye
    c. were Jewish Christians
    d. paid all of Paul's expenses
    e. all of the above

48. In Corinth, Paul
    a. preached every Sabbath in the synagogue
    b. was rejected by the Jews
    c. stayed with Titius Justus
    d. announced that from then he would go only to the Gentiles
    e. all of the above

49. Gallio, the Roman Governor of Achaia
    a. refused to judge Paul because of Paul's righteousness
    b. became converted and was baptized
    c. had Sosthenes beaten
    d. refused to judge Paul over a religious matter
    e. none of the above

50. At Ephesus
    a. Paul stayed with Aquila and Priscilla
    b. made a vow in the Jewish custom
    c. swore that he would return
    d. avoided the Jews completely
    e. all of the above

The Life and Ministry of Paul
Exam #2
Lessons Four through Eight

Multiple Choice:

1. Which, among the below, was not one of Apollos' qualifications?
    a. he was an eloquent speaker
    b. he had a thorough knowledge of the scriptures
    c. he had been instructed in the way of the Lord
    d. he knew the baptism of Jesus
    e. none of the above

2. Who explained to him more correctly the way of the Lord?
    a. Aquila and Priscilla
    b. Paul
    c. Luke
    d. Barnabas
    e. Alexandria

3. The problem with the twelve disciples from Ephesus was that they
    a. were Judaizers
    b. hadn't received the Holy Spirit
    c. hadn't been baptized in water
    d. hadn't heard of Jesus' baptism
    e. all of the above

4. When Paul placed his hands on the Ephesian disciples
    a. they were baptized in the name of Jesus
    b. the Holy Spirit came upon them
    c. they spoke in tongues
    d. they prophesied
    e. all of the above

5. At Ephesus, Paul
    a. spoke at the synagogue
    b. held discussions at the lecture hall of Tyrannus
    c. tried to convince people about the Kingdom of God
    d. performed miracles
    e. all of the above

6. The seven sons of Sceva
   a. were disciples of Paul
   b. opposed Paul's ministry
   c. were defeated by evil spirits
   d. prophesied against Ephesus
   e. none of the above

7. Paul's ministry in Ephesus was so strong that
   a. the governor of the province was saved
   b. over 10,000 people were converted to Christ
   c. many magicians burned their books in public
   d. the apostles sent observers from Jerusalem
   e. all of the above

8. Paul had planned to travel to
   a. Macedonia
   b. Achaia
   c. Jerusalem
   d. Rome
   e. all of the above

9. Paul sent Timothy to the Corinthians
   a. to remind them of Paul's teaching
   b. to collect the offering
   c. to rebuke evildoers there
   d. to relieve Titus who was ill
   e. all of the above

10. Demetrius caused Paul trouble in Ephesus by
    a. accusing Paul of being a Jew
    b. telling the goldsmiths that Paul was ruining them
    c. taking away his work permit
    d. stirring up a crowd to defend the goddess Artemis
    e. all of the above

11. Later, Paul recounted that in Ephesus he had
    a. served the Lord with humility
    b. endured hard times because of the Jews
    c. faced death every day
    d. been saved by God from the dangers of death
    e. all of the above

12. Concerning his teaching at Ephesus, Paul asserted that
    a. it was his fault if any were lost
    b. he had preached the Kingdom of God among them
    c. he had held back judgment from them
    d. everyone needs to be baptized to be saved
    e. all of the above

13. Concerning his manual labor, Paul said that
    a. pastors should not have to work with their hands
    b. it was a shame better provision wasn't made for him
    c. he had worked hard to be an example
    d. his blisters proved his faithfulness
    e. all of the above

14. The church in Macedonia
    a. was spared of persecution by the Lord
    b. was pastored by Apollos
    c. was generous, although poor
    d. wanted funds to construct a building
    e. all of the above

15. Paul was traveling to Jerusalem to
    a. deliver an offering to the church there
    b. confront Peter concerning his hypocrisy
    c. get credentials to preach from the apostles
    d. clear himself of charges made against him
    e. none of the above

16. At Troas
    a. Paul is joined again by Luke
    b. Paul ministered for a week
    c. Eutychus is raised up from the dead
    d. Paul avoided a Jewish plot
    e. all of the above

17. At Miletus the Ephesian elders cried because
    a. Paul warned them of hard times coming
    b. Paul asked for another offering
    c. Paul wouldn't allow them to go with him
    d. Paul said they would never see him again
    e. none of the above

18. When Paul arrived in Jerusalem
    a.   he went to see Peter
    b.   he greeted the elders and gave them a report
    c.   he was rejected by the brothers
    d.   he was immediately arrested
    e.   none of the above

19. Paul made a Jewish vow
    a.   to soothe the Jewish Christians' misunderstanding of his teaching
    b.   to disprove the bad report concerning his ministry
    c.   to prove that he kept the Jewish Law
    d.   to be obedient to the elders at Jerusalem
    e.   all of the above

20. Jews at the temple stirred up the crowd against Paul by
    a.   claiming Paul was uncircumcised
    b.   claiming Paul was trying to overthrow the Romans
    c.   claiming that Paul taught against the Jews, the Law and the temple
    d.   claiming Paul brought Timothy into the temple
    e.   all of the above

21. Paul was saved from the crowd at the temple when
    a.   an angel appeared and struck the people blind
    b.   he was arrested by the Roman soldiers
    c.   he shamed them with the Word of God
    d.   he spoke in Hebrew
    e.   none of the above

22. When Paul addressed the crowd at the Roman army barracks,   he
    a.   gave his testimony
    b.   told the Jews they would be rejected
    c.   spoke in Hebrew
    d   claimed he was innocent of wrongdoing
    e.   all of the above

23. When the centurion learned that Paul was a Roman citizen, he
    a.   said he had to pay for his citizenship
    b.   was alarmed he had put Paul in chains
    c.   stopped proceedings against Paul
    d.   decided not to flog Paul
    e.   all of the above

24. Before the Sanhedrin Paul created a controversy over the issue of
    a. baptism
    b. angels
    c. circumcision
    d. resurrection
    e. none of the above

25. Paul knew he would be going to Rome because
    a. the commander told him
    b. it had been prophesied
    c. the Lord told him in a vision
    d. he had received an invitation to the church there
    e. none of the above

26. Paul was moved to Caesarea because
    a. was a Jewish plot to ambush him
    b. Felix had asked to hear his case
    c. Paul appealed to Felix
    d. the jail in Jerusalem was overcrowded
    e. all of the above

27. The commander sent a letter to Governor Felix telling him
    a. about the Jewish plot
    b. that Paul was a Roman citizen
    c. that the Sanhedrin could give no real charge against him
    d. he wanted Paul's accusers to present their case to Felix
    e. all of the above

28. The charges brought against Paul by the Sanhedrin in the court of Felix included
    a. teaching against the Law of Moses
    b. not circumcising new converts
    c. not keeping the Sabbath
    d. not paying taxes
    e. none of the above

29. Paul said that the people who should be bringing charges against him were
    a. the Sanhedrin
    b. the Jews from Asia
    c. the Roman government
    d. Christians
    e. none of the above

30. Felix
    a. was well-acquainted with "the Way"
    b. listened to Paul with his wife Drusilla
    c. became afraid when Paul talked about the judgment
    d. kept Paul for two years hoping for a bribe from Paul
    e. all of the above

31. Porcius Festus
    a. wanted to do the Jews a favor
    b. listened to the charges against Paul
    c. agreed to Paul's appeal to Caesar
    d. didn't believe Paul was guilty of anything serious
    e. all of the above

32. Before King Agrippa, Paul
    a. told him he was a Sadducee
    b. claimed that the charges had to do with circumcision
    c. told him he was sent to warn the Jews of God's judgment
    d. testified about Jesus Christ
    e. all of the above

33. Agrippa asked Paul
    a. if he was trying to convert him to Christ
    b. why he was persecuting the Christians
    c. when he was going to pay the bribe
    d. what should he do to be saved
    e. none of the above

34. The "we" in Acts 27:1 concerning Paul's leaving for Rome indicates that
    a. more than one person wrote the Book of Acts
    b. Paul had been alone before that
    c. Luke was with Paul
    d. Paul wrote the Book of Acts
    e. none of the above

35. In Crete
    a. Paul was bitten by a viper
    b. Paul warned that the trip would be disastrous
    c. Paul was confined in prison
    d. the ship stayed at Phoenix
    e. all of the above

36. When a storm caught the ship, Paul told the men
    a. they should have listened to him
    b. none would be lost
    c. an angel had assured him everyone would be saved
    d. the ship would run aground
    e. all of the above

37. When the ship wrecked
    a. only the soldiers were killed
    b. only the sailors were killed
    c. everyone reached shore safely
    d. the prisoners escaped
    e. none of the above

38. People at Malta
    a. thought Paul was a god
    b. mistreated the survivors
    c. helped Paul escape
    d. started a church
    e. none of the above

39. While in Malta, Paul
    a. healed the chief official's father
    b. cured the sick people on the island
    c. was honored by the people
    d. was furnished with needed supplies
    e. all of the above

40. Arriving at Rome, Paul was encouraged when
    a. the ship finally docked
    b. the crew gave Paul a donation
    c. an angel assured him he would be released
    d. he saw the brothers coming to greet him
    e. none of the above

41. When Paul met at first with the Jews in Rome
    a. they had already been warned that he was a trouble maker
    b. they wanted to hear Paul's views
    c. most had already become Christians
    d. they refused to listen to him
    e. none of the above

42. After the Jews disagreed among themselves concerning Paul's teaching, he
    a. quoted Isaiah 6:9-10 to them
    b. said God's salvation had been sent to the Gentiles who would listen
    c. preached the Kingdom
    d. taught about Jesus Christ
    e. all of the above

43. Paul's son in the Lord was
    a. Timothy
    b. Epaphras
    c. Luke
    d. Philemon
    e. none of the above

44. If Paul's life and ministry closed with the end of the Book of Acts
    a. he could not be the author of the prison epistles
    b. he could not be the author of the pastoral epistles
    c. he would have to have been imprisoned for at least four years
    d. Luke must have died earlier
    e. all of the above

45. If Paul were imprisoned on two separate occasions in Rome, then
    a. he could have written the prison epistles during the first imprisonment
    b. he wrote Titus and 1 Timothy while free
    c. he wrote 2 Timothy during the final imprisonment
    d. the pastoral epistles contents make sense
    e. all of the above

46. Whom did Paul leave in Crete to appoint elders and oversee the churches there?
    a. Timothy
    b. Mark
    c. Titus
    d. Demas
    e. none of the above

47. Paul's enemies included the following except
    a. Alexander the coppersmith
    b. Hymenaeus
    c. Philetus
    d. Onesiphorus
    e. none of the above

48. Paul left Timothy to minister at
    a. Crete
    b. Ephesus
    c. Spain
    d. Corinth
    e. Rome

49. Paul's last charge to Timothy was for Timothy to
    a. re-fire his gift
    b. keep sound teaching with faith and love in Christ
    c. be strong in the grace of Jesus Christ
    d. to endure hardship
    e. all of the above

50. Paul told Timothy that in completing his mission he
    a. fought the good fight
    b. finished the race
    c. kept the faith
    d. was ready to receive the crown of righteousness as his reward
    e. all of the above

Made in United States
Troutdale, OR
06/29/2023

10872907R00075